THE K–3 GUIDE TO ACADEMIC CONVERSATIONS

THE K–3 GUIDE TO ACADEMIC CONVERSATIONS

Practices, Scaffolds, and Activities

Jeff Zwiers

Sara Hamerla

CORWIN

A SAGE Publishing Company

FOR INFORMATION:

Corwin

A SAGE Company

2455 Teller Road

Thousand Oaks, California 91320

(800) 233-9936

www.corwin.com

SAGE Publications Ltd.

1 Oliver's Yard

55 City Road

London, EC1Y 1SP

United Kingdom

SAGE Publications India Pvt. Ltd.

B 1/I 1 Mohan Cooperative Industrial Area

Mathura Road, New Delhi 110 044

India

SAGE Publications Asia-Pacific Pte. Ltd.

3 Church Street

#10-04 Samsung Hub

Singapore 049483

Program Director and Publisher: Dan Alpert

Associate Editor: Lucas Schleicher

Editorial Assistants: Katie Crilley
                        Mia Rodriguez

Production Editor: Tori Mirsadjadi

Copy Editor: Deanna Noga

Typesetter: C&M Digitals (P) Ltd.

Proofreader: Barbara Coster

Indexer: Scott Smiley

Cover Designer: Anupama Krishnan

Marketing Manager: Maura Sullivan

Printed in the United States of America

ISBN 978-1-5063-4041-8

This book is printed on acid-free paper.

SUSTAINABLE FORESTRY INITIATIVE
Certified Chain of Custody
Promoting Sustainable Forestry
www.sfiprogram.org
SFI-01268

SFI label applies to text stock

18 19 20 21 10 9 8 7 6 5 4 3

Contents

Visit the companion website at **resources.corwin.com/ZwiersK3Guide**
for videos and downloadable resources.

Image Credits: Chapter 1: iStock.com/monkeybusinessimages, Chapter 2: iStock.com/vgajic, Chapter 3: iStock.com/FatCamera,
Chapter 4: iStock.com/Tomwangll2, Chapter 5: iStock.com/kali9

Acknowledgments

We are grateful for the wonderful teachers with whom we have had the privilege to work. We especially thank Judy Flynn, Andrea Baer, Frank Rothwell, and Megan Quinlan of the Framingham Public Schools. Thank you to Kate Philipson of the Newton Public Schools. Credits to R. L. Sarafconn, who shared her creative ideas and artwork that she developed especially for kindergarten English learners. Thank you to Vanessa Sánchez of the Redwood City School District for her collaboration and insights.

About the Authors

Dr. Jeff Zwiers is a senior researcher at the Stanford University Graduate School of Education. He supports the Understanding Language Initiative, a research and professional development project focused on literacy, cognition, discourse, and academic language. His current research focuses on effective lesson planning and classroom practices that foster academic interactions and literacy.

Dr. Sara Hamerla is an ELL Administrator in the Newton Public Schools. She has taught English as a second language and served as an administrator in public schools in Massachusetts. Her teaching experience also includes teaching history and language arts in Colombia and Ecuador. In the past several years, she has taught many teachers how to implement academic conversations.

Introduction

Children's conversations are powerful sculptors of how they will think, build ideas, and relate to others throughout life.

Talking with others plays a major role in learning. When students engage in conversations, ideas are created, shaped, and shared. This can be even truer in primary grades because students first enter school and interact with a wide range of others who bring with them a wide range of ideas. Many young students talk plenty, but their conversation skills are largely underdeveloped. Some students get some modeling and practice at home, but many do not, and it is up to schools to help them.

This book is intended to be a practical guide for teachers who want to increase the quality and quantity of productive interactions in their classrooms. The benefits to students include higher-quality interpersonal engagement, increased motivation, development of negotiation and evaluation skills, and improved participation in small group collaborative learning, debates, and presentations.

WHAT ARE ACADEMIC CONVERSATIONS?

Conversations are back-and-forth interactions in which people share ideas and negotiate meaning through active listening and turn-taking. Academic conversations are sustained and purposeful conversations about school topics. While triads, small groups, and even whole class discussions can work, we tend to see more impact and engagement when practiced in pairs. A conversation between two students has many advantages in the primary grades. Young students can more easily focus on one peer and make eye contact while listening. We have all seen younger children engaging with a friend during play or free choice time. We have seen pairs creating Lego buildings, having "tea parties," and playing on a seesaw.

Paired conversations increase student talk in a lesson—at any given moment around half the students are producing language. And around half are listening and trying to comprehend input. Language used in real interactions (lots of input and output) is vital for developing language, social skills, and conceptual understandings in school and beyond. Paired conversations can firm up this foundation for students as they go through school so that they can participate more effectively in collaborative work, whole class discussions, debates, and presentations. They can also apply these skills at home with their families and later in life in the workplace.

We have been inspired by the many reports from teachers on how academic conversations are already happening in a variety of classrooms. From conversations about energy in fourth grade to conversations about short stories in tenth grade, a wide range of teachers have succeeded at weaving conversations and their skills into lessons. Yet many primary grade teachers have noticed that their students need extra support that isn't covered in other books and most resources focused on conversations. So we began to work more closely with primary grade teachers who were excited to help contribute to a resource that would help young students develop skills for engaging in more productive conversations.

For thousands of years people have been using the skills in this book to engage in conversations with others. What isn't as prevalent, however, is teaching students—especially in primary grades—to engage in productive conversations about academic ideas. Fortunately, many teachers around the country have realized this need, due in part to new content and English language

Conversations foster authentic uses of language in real time.

development standards, to teach students to and through talk. Many schools are beginning to teach conversation skills and gathering exciting evidence of the increases in both quantity and quality of student interactions.

THE BENEFITS OF CONVERSING IN SCHOOL

Many researchers have discussed the importance of engaging students in conversations to learn. A growing body of literature on oral language in the classroom (e.g., Fisher, Frey, & Rothenberg, 2008; Goldenberg, 1992; McIntyre, Kyle, & Moore, 2006; Wasik & Iannone-Campbell, 2012) has focused on the importance of teacher-student dialogue for learning content and vocabulary. However, few studies have shown how students can learn to converse with peers by employing communication skills (Cole, 2003; Zwiers & Soto, 2016) and how academic conversations help students acquire language structures beyond the word level. There is little research on peer conversations in elementary classrooms and even less on English learners, a population that benefits greatly from oral language opportunities during instruction.

To learn how to participate effectively and independently in conversations, students need lots of modeling, scaffolding, and practice. Teachers of younger students need to help them build five core communication skills: listen actively, create, clarify, support ideas, and evaluate (Zwiers, O'Hara, & Pritchard, 2014). Through focused instruction in these core conversation skills and with scaffolds (such as visuals, hand gestures, and sentence starters), students are able to extend and deepen their conversations. New vocabulary and syntax can be incorporated into discussions, so students become more independent thinkers, and they learn to explore important themes rather than just retelling their ideas.

Children increasingly use screens to communicate. This lack of face-to-face conversation has changed the quality of interactions between people. Clearly, technology can facilitate long-distance communications and workplace decisions. However, when people are face-to-face, they must engage with others in conversation, which includes active listening, empathy, sharing, negotiating, and building ideas. We have noticed that in recent decades schools have neglected to teach students how to talk with one another about academic topics. It is our goal to change the classroom dynamic and help students regain their voices, starting in the early years of schooling.

When students build up ideas with a partner, they often learn new information from that person. They also learn about that person and build relationships. These relationships are especially important for English language learners who need many and varied opportunities to produce language. Many shy students also build confidence as they talk with partners of various proficiency levels during the year.

Academic conversations provide young English learners an opportunity to grow and try out new ways of using language to describe ideas. Students are also introduced to sociocultural norms of communication in the United States, such as making eye contact, using gestures, asking clarifying questions, respectfully disagreeing. If these norms and skills are not addressed and practiced in primary grades, students can fall dangerously behind as they enter upper grades.

Finally, the emphasis on academic conversations in one of our focal schools (Brophy Elementary) also contributed to exceptional growth in scores on the English language proficiency test (ACCESS by WIDA). Among second graders at the school, for example, the average speaking scores were one full level higher than scores at other schools with similar populations in the district. Administrators and teachers also noticed the overall positive impact of academic conversations on student learning. When students were participating in academic conversations during these observations, it was easier to see evidence of students articulating their thinking, explaining how they solve problems, and overall engaging in learning.

A BRIEF BACKGROUND AND RATIONALE

As most teachers know all too well, first graders and fifth graders are *very* different, particularly in how they think and interact with others. So, as we applied and tried ideas to foster conversations, we developed a significant number of tools and strategies to match the developmental needs of diverse primary grade students in our settings. For example, we worked with teachers to develop focused listening skills alongside the other skills. We created anchor charts with colorful visuals and sentence frames. We engaged in action research focused on academic conversations in primary grades. We then shared with each other and with other colleagues how we were teaching and what we were learning. This book is the result of these conversations about conversations.

This book is also a response to the many primary grade teachers who have asked for lesson plans, anchor charts, scaffolds, protocols, and practical ideas for improving the conversations in the first years of schooling. As we worked with teachers and thought about sharing what we learned, six main objectives for the book emerged. After reading it, educators will be able to

- Argue the importance of developing conversation skills and oral language in primary grades, especially in English learners, many of whom do not receive any extra help in English

- Develop academic conversation skills in content area lessons in early grades

- Use conversations to teach academic content, skills, and language required by standards

- Design anchor charts with questions and response starters appropriate for younger learners

- Analyze transcripts of student conversations and determine areas of need

- Engage families and communities as partners in developing conversation skills

The chapters in this book provide a window into the practical applications of academic conversations. Chapters include anchor charts, sample lesson plans that can be adapted, and suggested activities. Authentic conversation transcripts are interspersed throughout. These transcripts provide an opportunity to "hear" what actual students might say to each other. Teachers can informally assess these conversations and determine next steps for instruction. Throughout the book, we anticipate challenges and provide tips for teaching the core skills. We also explain how to craft powerful conversation prompts that inspire deep thinking among students. Each chapter ends with professional learning community (PLC) prompts that can be used as conversation starters in PLCs or other professional development.

Chapter 1: Building a Foundation for Conversation Work provides an overview for setting up a culture of conversation in primary classrooms, along with a case study of a second grade classroom that illustrates how academic conversations can be introduced. In *Chapter 2: Activities and Lesson Plans for Introducing the Skills,* five core conversation skills are explained. Each skill is accompanied by a gesture, icon, and anchor chart with questions and responses starters. Sample lesson plans and activities are included. The next two chapters address academic conversations in the content areas. *Chapter 3: Academic Conversations for Literacy* explains adaptations for literacy instruction, including readers' and writers' workshops, while *Chapter 4: Academic Conversations in Science, Social Studies, Math, and Art* covers ways to support different types of conversations in these content areas. *Chapter 5: Assessing Student Conversations* helps teachers assess academic conversations using the Conversation Observation and Analysis Tool (COAT), and it includes suggestions for peer and student self-assessment of conversations.

The appendices include suggestions for family engagement, professional development, and FAQs. Appendix B also includes a link to online videos and other tools. The videos provide a glimpse into the language production of actual students and provide a chance for teachers to practice listening carefully to language and skill use within conversations.

Teachers in a variety of educational settings have found that students learn more deeply when they create ideas through conversations. We have seen that, given an early and strong start in conversing about academic topics in productive ways, students are far more poised to succeed in upper elementary and beyond. Oral language development is especially important for culturally and linguistically diverse students. As young children collaborate with peers to clarify, build on and support ideas, and evaluate and compare important points, they use language as a tool for communicating thinking. Academic conversations have changed the dynamic in the classrooms of teachers we have supported. We hope you will be willing to embrace this approach and the powerful changes that will result.

PLC PROMPTS FOCUSED ON THE PURPOSE
OF ACADEMIC CONVERSATIONS

- Think about your early memories engaging in conversations. What were the expectations at the dinner table at home? What were the topics of conversations? What language was spoken at home?

- How did these experiences change during your days in primary grades at school? Middle school? High school? If you will, compare your experiences growing up with those of today's youth. What do you know about how preteens and teenagers converse in school? Outside of school?

BUILDING A FOUNDATION FOR CONVERSATION WORK

Rome wasn't built in one conversation.

Imagine you are listening to this conversation between two third graders during readers' workshop. The prompt is "Should we have zoos or not?" Students had read a short article and the pros and cons of zoos. Think about if and why this conversation is a good use of precious class time.

Ernesto: I think we should have zoos.

Diana: Why?

Ernesto: Cuz they're fun. And then you get to see animals.

Diana: Yeah. I like to see the gorillas.

Ernesto: Why do you like them?

Diana: They play on things, and, I don't know.

Ernesto: So you think zoos are good?

Diana: Yep. But like the teacher said, I wonder if the animals like it.

Ernesto: What do you mean?

Diana: They are in cages and can't get out. And lots of people watch them, like, all day.

Ernesto: Yeah, I agree. And sometimes they look sad or bored. But they also get free food, like, not have to find it, or like hunt things.

Diana: So zoos are good and bad?

Ernesto: I guess.

Diana: OK. We're done.

We would argue that this conversation is worth the time. Notice the purposeful uses of language used by these two students. They are using language to collaboratively build ideas, and they are using conversation skills that will serve them now and in the future. But how did they get to this point? We start with a brief overview of the five main academic conversation skills (which we cover more in depth in the next chapter). Then we highlight the challenging, yet integral process of building a conversation culture in the classroom.

ACADEMIC CONVERSATION SKILLS

Three of the four main conversation skills focus on building up one idea. These are creating and/or posing, clarifying, and supporting an idea with examples and evidence. Every conversation should build up at least one idea. Posing an idea means putting a relevant and useful idea on the table to build up. Clarifying means to make sure both students are on a similar page with respect to the meaning of the idea. Often they will define, elaborate, negotiate meanings, or even use analogies to clarify. The fourth skill, evaluating, is needed if the conversation is argumentative, meaning that there are two or more ideas built up and there is a need to choose one (Zwiers & Soto, 2016).

The fifth skill is focused listening, which is "cross-cutting" in that it is needed by the other four skills (see Figure 1.1). In fact, many teachers notice that if students don't listen (Do you have any students with this challenge?), conversations can't build up ideas. Speaking is also needed (and could be a sixth skill), but this skill is fostered by working on the skill of clarifying.

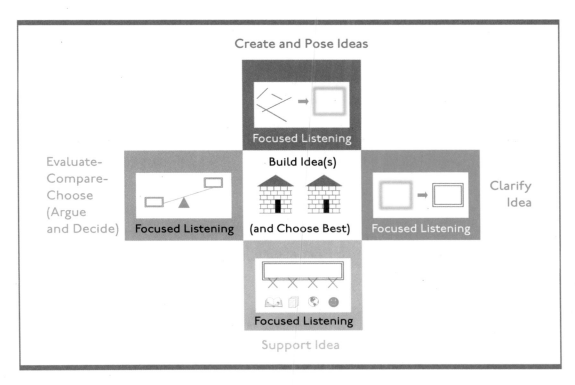

Figure 1.1 Academic Conversation Skills

 resources.corwin.com/ZwiersK3Guide

Gestures for the Skills. A fun and effective way to help students remember and use these skills is with hand gestures. For posing, you can put one hand out, palm up. For clarifying, you make "binoculars" with both hands and put them up to your eyes. For supporting, you put your hand back out, palm up, and then bring the thumb and fingers of the other hand up underneath it to support it. And for evaluating, comparing, and choosing, you put each arm out to your side, palm up, and move them up and down like a balance scale. For focused listening, you put a hand behind one ear and nod your head.

BUILDING A CONVERSATION CULTURE

Conversations will not take root unless there is a solid ground of "conversation culture" in the classroom. This culture is built in a variety of ways by different teachers, but the best examples are classrooms with students who know what the cultural norms are and why they exist, peer- and self-reflect on how well they are following the norms, have lots of chances to practice the norms in real conversations, and have a teacher who observes and provides feedback focused on the norms.

A great example of building a conversation culture is Judy Flynn's second-grade classroom. Judy collaborated with her learning team members to analyze data from student achievement. They designed an inquiry question: How can we increase the quality of academic language in conversations? The data team then developed a plan for classroom and schoolwide implementation of academic conversations. A key part of the plan was working hard to foster a conversation-based culture in every lesson.

She started with an introductory lesson with an anchor chart: "What is an academic conversation?" It included features that were and were not appropriate for academic conversations (see Figure 1.2).

Academic Conversation	
What it is	**What it isn't**
Being respectful	Being disrespectful
Sitting correctly	Slouching or wiggling around
Making eye contact	Looking around the room
Listening to each other	Not listening or daydreaming
Being serious	Acting silly
Staying on topic	Talking on anything you want
Using appropriate language	Using slang or language for recess

Courtesy of Judy Flynn

Figure I.2   Anchor Chart for Introducing Academic Conversations in Second Grade

In her initial lessons, Judy started to teach the main conversation skills. But she quickly also saw that students weren't listening well enough to maintain attention for using the main skills. So she developed several short lessons on focused listening. Students first practiced facing one another with their whole bodies and engaged posture. Next, Judy modeled smiling, nodding, and making eye contact. She then modeled negative versions of these to show how one feels when a partner isn't listening. Finally, she modeled listening with the purpose of getting the gist of what the person is saying. She said, "Sure, you can fake all these things and look like you are listening, but you need to listen to know what to say next. You can't fake it once you start talking."

Courtesy of R.L. Sarafconn

Figure 1.3　　Conversation Skills Anchor Chart
for an English Language Development Classroom

online resources　resources.corwin.com/ZwiersK3Guide

Judy and other teachers also realized that students needed extra practice saying utterances that showed focused listening. So the teachers asked students to also say things like, "Uh huh." "I see." "Interesting!" "Really?" "Hmmm." "And then?" and "Wow!" At first the students giggled, but they all were engaged and understood the value of these little utterances, especially because others used them while they were speaking to show understanding.

Judy also strategically paired students for the conversations. Often English learners would be paired with native English speakers, and at other times students were paired with peers of similar proficiency. Students learned about their friends, developed deeper relationships, strengthened their identity as learners, and developed self-confidence from having their ideas validated by peers.

In classrooms with English learners at the more beginning and emerging levels of proficiency, you can use a chart like the one shown in Figure 1.3. Notice the power of the images for reminding students of key norms and skills.

CONVERSATION AS A FOUNDATION OF TEACHING AND LEARNING

As you saw in the case study, teachers can use a variety of tools and strategies to get started in building a conversation-based culture. But for learning to happen and conversations to thrive, there needs to be a pedagogical "foundation of conversation." This means a classroom where conversation supports learning in the beginnings, middles, and ends of lessons and units. It means students expect to talk deeply and thoroughly about topics to understand the ideas better and to understand the varying perspectives of classmates. It means teachers who value talk, appreciate its messy and loud nature, and work to help students improve their skills at talking about a wide range of topics with a wide range of people.

Why is this foundation so important? Because if students during four crucial years of learning (Grades K through 3) start to think that learning is simply memorizing facts to earn good grades or please the teacher, then this is what they will tend to believe learning is for the rest of their schooling. If the foundation of learning is quantity, or counting up points on individual quizzes, tests, and assignments, then students don't see the need to develop collaboration skills.

Setting Up the Foundation

1. The first week of school tell students that they will be talking a lot to other students in back-and-forth academic conversations. Model conversations with students and/or other adults.

2. Demonstrate a model of nonacademic, "wrong way" conversations, immediately followed by the "right way" to have a conversation. This is your chance to be an actor! Enlist one of your students to model with you. Prep him or her quietly in advance on how to act out a nonacademic conversation. For example:

Teacher: Hey, what up?

Student: *(Looking down at the ground)* What are we supposed to be talking about?

Teacher: Books, I think.

Student: What did you do last weekend?

3. Ask students, "What did you notice about this conversation?" (They should reply, "No eye contact." "Got off topic." "Didn't build up an idea.")

4. Immediately follow with a positive model of an academic conversation. Be sure to use the same volunteer student actor so he or she will physically practice the correct way. For example:

Teacher: What book did you find interesting this summer?

Student: The book about dinosaurs was interesting.

Teacher: What made it interesting?

Student: It's about a boy who goes to a museum and sees dinosaur fossils.

Teacher: I see. And what about the fossils? What did he or you learn?

Student: That you can learn a lot about how they lived from the bones. What about you?

Teacher: I read a book about a boy who was born on the moon. It was in the future. I learned that we might do mining on the moon some day.

5. Ask students, "What did you notice about this conversation?" (They should reply, "You were both smiling, nodding, and making eye contact." "You stayed on topic." "You listened." "You built on each other's ideas.")

6. Strategically teach conversation skills. Emphasize that over the course of the year, you will gradually have students take more control of discussions and not rely on you for all things conversation. Explain that each skill is a "double skill"—"You will be able to use the skill, and you will help your partner use the skill. For example, you will clarify an idea and you will ask

questions to your partner to help him or her clarify an idea." Students will have anchor charts to use as resources.

7. Be sure to craft carefully worded prompts to begin engaging in conversations and teach students how to end a conversation politely.

8. Plan conversations in all subject areas throughout the day. When students speak to communicate to others (not just for points), they are developing oracy that will support literacy. Young children, especially, need intensive oral language practice with content area concepts to strengthen their language for early literacy development.

9. Show students how you will monitor and help students to become better at conversation. You can tell students that, because you value their conversations with one another, you will observe them and provide feedback to help them become better conversationalists during the year. Along the way you will also ask them to self-assess their own progress in the area of conversations.

COMING UP WITH EFFECTIVE CONVERSATION PROMPTS

One of the common requests in our work with teachers is help with crafting effective prompts for student conversations. Good prompts cannot be crafted on the fly, and most curriculum materials try to provide them, but they are often too generic. A good prompt is often based on the most interesting ideas or information stemming from a current text or topic of study. It also takes into account your students' interests and background knowledge (which is why most published teacher's guides don't cut it). Here are some other criteria of effective prompts:

- **They have engaging and authentic purposes.** Even though many young students like to talk just to be talking, they need to be apprenticed into conversing on academic topics. We don't want students simply filling time with talk or going through the motions of conversations to make you happy; we want them to do interesting and academic things with their interactions.

- **They consider the different ideas and skills that students can share with one another.** This includes taking into account and leveraging the different knowledge and skills that students must share with each other to accomplish the conversation's purpose.

- **They are clear and focused.** They set students up with enough information to focus on or generate appropriate ideas.

- **They provide opportunities and support for using new language, content, and thinking.**

Less effective and incomplete prompts	Effective prompts
In your conversation, talk about the book.	What do you think we are supposed to learn from the main character in this book? Use parts of the story to support your ideas.
Describe the polar bear to each other.	How do adaptations help the polar bear survive in its habitat? I would like to hear you use sentences like this one, "If a polar bear didn't . . . , it probably wouldn't survive because . . ."
Discuss this math problem and how to solve it.	Work with your partner to come up with two ways to solve this problem. Ask each other "why" questions as you talk to explain why you are choosing to do certain things. For example . . .
In your conversation, summarize what you read about your famous historical person.	With your partner, come up with a description of how to be a famous person in history. I want to be famous. What do I need to do? What do I need to say? What kind of personality do I need? Use the stories you read. And don't forget to ask your partner to clarify, if he or she doesn't say enough.

As you can see by the examples on the right, effective prompts (a) allow students to share what they know and to shape ideas with partners, without being too "loosey goosey," so to speak, and (b) are more work to create. But you will quickly see positive results as you work on beefing up your prompts in these ways.

CHAPTER SUMMARY

This chapter has introduced the basics of academic conversations and a rationale for implementing them on a daily basis in primary settings. The next chapter includes anchor charts and lessons that illustrate how teachers can build students' abilities to communicate through active listening, creating, clarifying, supporting ideas, and evaluating.

PLC PROMPTS FOCUSED ON SETTING THE FOUNDATION

- How would academic conversations help you assess if students are meeting the language and content objectives in your classroom?

- Consider your school and district. What systems are in place to support schoolwide change? Does the data at your site indicate that there is a need for more academic language?

ACTIVITIES AND LESSON PLANS FOR INTRODUCING THE SKILLS

Much like the winds sculpt the mountains, conversations sculpt our minds.

We recommend that you introduce each of the five skills individually, using familiar content, and that you allow plenty of time for modeling and practicing of the skill. Each skill can be presented to students with a simple icon and gesture. And we encourage you to think about how you can adapt the suggestions in this book to your own student population.

Along with an explanation of each skill, in this chapter you will find sample anchor charts, sample lesson plans (including key vocabulary phrases and language functions), and activities for reinforcing skills. Before introducing the skills, begin by creating an evolving class definition of academic conversations. What makes a conversation academic or not? Have students try to think of skills, and if they don't generate them, describe and model the skills for students.

DEVELOPING THE CROSS-CUTTING SKILL: FOCUSED LISTENING

As teachers, we would often remind our students, "Be good listeners." "Pay attention." Or "Show me the school listening look." Slowly we realized saying these things was not enough. We needed to provide them with hefty amounts of modeling and practice to grow both the physical (body and eyes) and cognitive (comprehending the gist to respond) sides of listening.

Smiling, nodding, and making eye contact are three visual cues that show listening in academic settings. These things, as you know, may not be practiced in the same ways across cultures. However, research on interactions between young children and caregivers has demonstrated the importance of this practice, particularly in preparing students for interacting in U.S. schools and job settings. Making eye contact builds trust and even supports early brain development (Farroni, Csibra, Simion, & Johnson, 2002). Smiling and nodding are gestures that indicate positive feelings and also contribute to a feeling of safety and trust.

Figure 2.1 is an anchor chart to remind students of key physical aspects of listening.

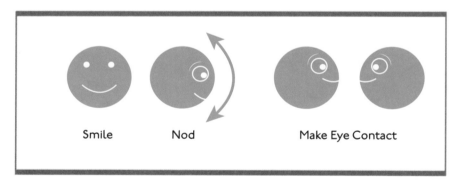

Smile   Nod   Make Eye Contact

Figure 2.1   Anchor Chart for Active Listening

online resources | resources.corwin.com/ZwiersK3Guide

When practicing listening, we model for the students the importance of the three actions and explain, "In the United States, making eye contact, nodding, and smiling indicate attention." Then we ask one student in each pair to answer easy prompts, while listeners practice the listening actions. The next step for this practice is to add some short "listening lingo" utterances (a.k.a. backchannels) such as "Oh really." "Um hum." "Wow!" and "Interesting." Both students practice these while also doing the physical movements as they listen to one another. While it may seem awkward at first, students see how this can show others that they are listening to them.

Of course, good listening involves much more than actions and interjections. Students need to focus on and understand what is said by another to make meaning or ask for clarification that helps the conversation. Many children (and adults) have learned to nod, smile, and so on while not understanding a single thing. A student might be able to listen for key information

---

During and After Listening to My Partner:

Am I understanding what my partner is saying?
Can I summarize it in one sentence?

Does what my partner is saying help to support and build up the current idea? Does it argue against the current idea?

Does what my partner is saying help to clarify the current idea?

Figure 2.2   Anchor Chart for Focused Listening

 resources.corwin.com/ZwiersK3Guide

in a short lecture on volcanoes, but it is a different skill to listen to a partner talk about volcanoes *every other turn* and use the information in each turn to craft one's own responses that ultimately build up an idea. Throughout the next sections covering conversation skills, we describe how listening plays a key role in each.

Turn-Taking

An important skill that depends on good listening is taking appropriate turns. This is especially needed in primary grades because of students' lack of experience, patience, and focus. Of course, the first thing students need to know and have modeled for them is that conversations involve multiple turns by each student. One part of the skill is knowing when to take the turn. Student A must listen to see if Student B is finishing his or her turn and wants to let Student A talk. Another part is knowing when and how to interrupt, if needed. Students also need to realize that they can't just be the interviewer and ask short questions. This is needed at times, but each student must share ideas, clarifications, evidence, opinions, evaluations, and so on.

One way to develop turn-taking prowess is with **Turn-Taking Counters** (TTCs). Students are given three to six counters (chips). When conversing with a partner, a student can slide a counter forward on her table each time she takes a turn. You can also use different colors for different types of turns.

Manipulatives can help support turn-taking
and other conversation skills.

For example, if the student prompts for clarification or evidence, she slides a yellow chip in. If she poses an idea, clarifies, supports, or evaluates an idea in her turn, she puts a red counter in.

ASSESSING LISTENING

Use the following rubric to assess the cross-cutting skill of focused listening.

Table 2.1   Listening: Formative Assessment Tool

Criteria	Below Standard	Approaching	At or Exceeds
Listening comprehension	Little or no observation of building on partner ideas and requests for clarification; little or no evidence of listening.	The majority of the time, builds on partner ideas, asks for clarification, and paraphrases partner ideas to show listening.	Builds on partner ideas, asks for clarification, and paraphrases partner ideas to show effective listening.
Use of appropriate nonverbal behaviors (active listening)	Partners seldom use appropriate postures, movements, and eye contact to show engagement and listening.	Partners use some appropriate postures, movements, and eye contact to show engagement and listening.	Partners use appropriate postures, movements, and eye contact to show engagement and listening.

DEVELOPING CONVERSATION SKILL 1: CREATE OR POSE A RELEVANT IDEA TO BUILD UP

Creating or posing an idea is the first conversation skill for obvious reasons. It gets the conversation rolling. And the difference between good and not-so-good initial ideas have a major impact on the quality of the conversation.

Many primary students need to learn to create or pose relevant, objective-serving ideas in their conversations with peers. Easier written than said, right? This anchor chart (Figure 2.3) provides an illustration of the term "create." Students can refer to this anchor chart when initiating conversations and to construct questions and responses during conversations.

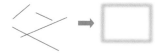

Create and Pose Ideas

State an idea that solves a problem, finds a pattern, or gives an opinion.

Questions:	Responses:
What is your idea?	One idea is . . .
What does it remind you of?	That reminds me of . . .

Figure 2.3   Anchor Chart for Create and Pose

 resources.corwin.com/ZwiersK3Guide

Students need practice posing "buildable" and valuable ideas in the classroom. Through well-crafted lessons and activities, teachers can model how to share and then refine ideas that foster learning of language and content objectives. During guided practice, students connect with partners and take turns developing ideas while learning content. Teachers must design tasks that engage students in observing, problem solving, finding patterns, and creating hypotheses during math lessons, literacy blocks, science, social studies, and unified arts.

Sample Lesson Plan for Developing Academic Conversation Skills: Creating and Posing Ideas

This lesson plan can be modified according to the grade level and language proficiency levels of the students. The three values are schoolwide values from a specific school and can be changed according to the context. There are essential components of the lesson including the introduction and multiple reviews of the CREATE and POSE anchor chart, gestures, and questions with responses.

Grades: K–3

Standards Addressed

CCSS.ELA-LITERACY.SL.2.I: Participate in collaborative conversations with diverse partners about grade level topics and texts with peers and adults in small and larger groups.

Objectives

- Describe one of the three values (Be respectful. Be responsible. Be prepared.) using cause and effect academic terms ("When a student is respectful, then . . .").
- Develop Conversation Skill: Create and Pose Ideas.
- Ask a partner to share an idea and explain ("What is your idea?" "Why?").
- Connect an idea to a more important concept ("For example . . .").

Performance Assessment

Paired conversation between two students analyzed with the Conversation Observation and Analysis Tool (COAT); (see Chapter 5).

Text

Teachers and students create text together by illustrating a series of visuals depicting students exhibiting core values.

Lesson Sequence

Introduce skill, build background, and create an idea

- Introduce language and content objectives.
- Build background—Remind students about three school values. What do they look like? Sound like? Feel like? (Make charts if needed.)

- Show a slideshow with visuals of examples and non-examples illustrating "respect." At each visual, ask students, "Does this show respect? Turn and ask your partner, 'Does this show respect?'"

- Teach the gesture and icon for "create an idea" using the CREATE and POSE anchor chart. This week we will be practicing "creating an idea that is conversation-worthy."

- "I want you to think of our big questions: How do our school values help us learn more? Which value do you think is most important for helping us learn?"

- Explain that you will model the nonacademic conversation (wrong way) with a student (no eye contact, off topic).

- Ask for feedback: What did you notice when we modeled the nonacademic conversation?

- Model the *academic* conversation (correct way) with a student. Model the posing of a conversation-worthy idea (e.g., I think respect is the most important for learning because . . .)

- Ask for feedback: What did you notice when we modeled the academic conversation?

- Academic conversation practice in pairs. Which value do you think is most important for helping us learn? Why?

Review and Assessment

Use the COAT to assess the skill.

Informal teacher analysis of use of language at the word and sentence levels during conversations.

Extension or Home-School Connection

Students have an academic conversation at home with a family member: Which value is important in your life? Why?

Report back to class on answers.

ACTIVITIES FOR BUILDING
THE SKILL OF CREATING/POSING

- **Think-Pair-Shares.** Pair-shares, turn-n-talks, and the like tend to be good activities for practicing the posing of ideas. Indeed, this type of practice is what these activities are best at. But with some extra structure.

- **Target Cards.** Pairs are given a green "topic card" with the topic or objective for a lesson or unit. They also receive blue "idea cards." These are printed with a wide range of relevant and irrelevant ideas that might be posed by people. Students put the green topic card in the middle of the target and then take turns drawing a blue idea card and reading it. They both then place it on an image of a target and discuss how they determined if it belongs in the bulls-eye, on the next concentric ring, or out of range. The placement of the idea card on the image of the target depends on how relevant it is to the topic. This can later lead to brainstorm sessions in which students pose their own ideas on cards and then place them on a target.

- **Language Experience Approach** (LEA). The teacher transcribes students' oral production into an expository or narrative written record on chart paper. The key to an effective language experience approach is a comprehensible, common experience shared by the class. The common experience could be an activity, text, field trip, experiment, or discovery in science. The sequence of events in history or steps to solve a math problem can also be recorded into an LEA. A read-aloud of a mentor text could be used as long as the text is comprehensible to all students. While recording students' ideas, the teacher explicitly models academic vocabulary usage and language structure. Teachers can prerecord target language structures as paragraph frames to structure talk and writing. The creative text can then be a stepping-off point for the editing process.

- **Parking Lot.** Create a "parking lot" where students can write down ideas, at any time, that might be useful later. You or they can then look at the parking lot for conversation ideas, when appropriate. Even the act of writing ideas down and posting them can help students remember their ideas longer.

- **Assessing the Skill of Creating and Posing Ideas in Conversations**

  You can formatively assess students' abilities to pose relevant ideas by observing and using the COAT (see Chapter 5). You can also use a basic checklist for evaluating the skill:

  o   Does the idea relate to the lesson objectives?

  o   Does the idea allow for explanation and elaboration?

  o   Does the idea involve opinion or have alternative perspectives?

DEVELOPING CONVERSATION
SKILL 2: CLARIFY IDEAS

One of the highlights of teaching primary grades is the chance to be an integral part of helping students learn how to describe their ideas to others. Each child has a fascinating and rich mix of ideas, words, and grammar. As they share their ideas and get feedback from others (like a confused look), they gradually learn how to put ideas into words and sentences to get their ideas across. Conversations with others are perfect settings in which to practice and improve oral language. They get to practice putting their ideas into words, and they get to hear how others put ideas into words.

Once students have a relevant idea posed, they need to clarify it. Clarifying is a "double skill" in that students need to both clarify their own ideas and prompt their partners to clarify. Students must listen to partners while partners share—and when they share, they must read the signs of confusion on partners' faces. They must grapple with a variety of communication styles and linguistic strategies used by student partners. Students can use a variety of "moves" to clarify ideas:

Ask questions ("Why did you say that? How did that happen? When . . .")

Define a term used ("Can you tell me what you mean by 'friend'?")

Elaborate on a basic, cliché, or overly terse idea ("Tell me more about how you think volcanoes form.") Often, a student will respond in a statement without much detail, for example, "Samantha is the most important character." Younger students can prompt for elaboration by saying, "Tell me more about . . ." It is important to teach older students to say, "Can you elaborate on . . . ," rather than just "Can you elaborate?" because this forces the asker to pick out a certain part of what the speaker has said and give it a name. For example, "Can you elaborate on why she is important?" (See the anchor chart on page 33 for an example of how to model this move.)

Paraphrase ("So what you are saying is that cats are the best pets because they are smart?") Paraphrasing involves listening to one or more partner turns and condensing its meaning back to the partner to see if you understood the meaning or direction of the message. Paraphrasing requires and inspires good listening. Often in life, one needs to remember key information from longer stretches of listening. Purposes for paraphrasing include:

- To keep track of what you are hearing

- To organize the speaker's points

- To describe in your own words

- To negotiate meaning: The listener synthesizes main points and the speaker affirms if that was the intended message

- To help the speaker and the conversation stay on topic

- To chunk ideas: The listener will improve in listening and reading comprehension

Courtesy of R.L Sarafconn

Figure 2.4　　　　　　　　　Anchor Chart for Paraphrasing

When young children first practice paraphrasing, their language may sound unnatural. They preface their paraphrasing by saying, "I understand, you said . . ." or "In other words . . ." or "So what you are saying is . . ." However, over time, they gain a larger repertoire of responses and will sound more fluent as they paraphrase their partner in appropriate, natural phrases.

If you say . . .	I'll paraphrase . . .
Animals need like lots of stuff to live, like air, water, food, and maybe a house or home. The things that grow, you know, plants, need all that and light.	So what you're saying is all living things need air, water, and food or nutrients. Animals need shelter or protection, and plants need light.
I think it is more better to live in a city than a town because there is more to see and do and more people there living all in big buildings and lots of cars.	So you think that living in a city is better than living in a town. One reason is that there are different activities. Also, there is more housing and transportation.
In this story all the kids come over in a rainbow-colored station wagon. They pull up in front of the house, jump out, and hug everyone from the kitchen to the living room. All summer they tended the garden and ate up all the strawberries and melons. They play lots of musical instruments. When they finally left, everyone was sad. But they knew the relatives would be back next summer.	The story is about a loving family. When the relatives drive up to visit, they jump out of their car and hug everyone. The family spends the summer together eating, playing, and making music.

Negotiate meanings ("OK, let's agree that love means you do good stuff for others.")

Use analogies and visuals ("This guy is like that bug that didn't work in the story about the ants. The bug got hungry, too." "Here, I'll draw what I mean for you.")

Here is an anchor chart that can help as you model and teach the skill.

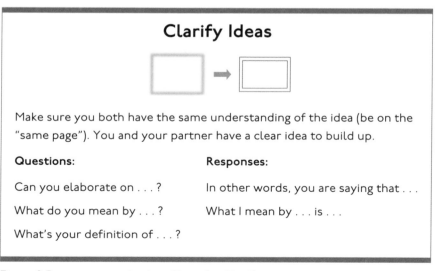

Clarify Ideas

Make sure you both have the same understanding of the idea (be on the "same page"). You and your partner have a clear idea to build up.

Questions:

Can you elaborate on . . . ?

What do you mean by . . . ?

What's your definition of . . . ?

Responses:

In other words, you are saying that . . .

What I mean by . . . is . . .

Figure 2.5   Anchor Chart for Clarify

Figure 2.6   Anchor Chart for Elaborate

online resources   resources.corwin.com/ZwiersK3Guide

Sample Lesson Plan for Developing Academic Conversation Skills: Clarifying

In this lesson plan, students are introduced to the academic conversation skill of CLARIFY. The routine is similar to the routine used in CREATE and POSE. The essential components of the lesson include the introduction and multiple reviews of the CLARIFY anchor chart, gestures, and questions with responses. The teacher will teach key words, phrases, and target language structures for determining the theme (or lesson of the story). This lesson plan can be modified according to the grade level and language proficiency levels of the students.

Grade: I

Standards Addressed

CCSS.ELA-LITERACY.SL.2.3: Ask and answer questions about what a speaker says to clarify comprehension, gather additional information, or deepen understanding of a topic or issue.

Objectives

Ask a partner to clarify an idea ("Should the little red hen have shared her bread with the other animals?")

Performance Assessment

Paired conversations about the theme of sharing from the story *The Little Red Hen*.

Lesson Sequence

Introduce skill, build background, and clarify an idea

- Introduce language and content objectives.

- Build background—Remind students about learning lessons from stories (Text: The Little Red Hen).

- Teach the word "clarify".

- Teach the gesture and icon for "clarify" with a CLARIFY anchor chart.

- "This week we will be practicing 'clarify an idea.' An idea should be clear, and make sense. If our friends don't understand, we need to explain our thinking or elaborate and tell more about our idea. If I want to be sure I understand a friend's idea, I can ask him or her to explain more or elaborate."

- Fishbowl modeling: Teacher and a student introduce prompt: "What is the lesson to be learned from reading this story? Should we act like the hen?"

Student:	I think yes. The other animals didn't help.
Teacher:	Can you say more about your reason?
Student:	If they didn't help, they don't get the bread. She asked them to help but they don't help her.
Teacher:	So you are saying that they could have helped and didn't, so they don't deserve to eat?
Student:	Yeah. They're lazy.
Teacher:	What does that mean?
Student:	When you don't work.
Teacher:	Can you give an example?
Student:	Like when I don't clean my room. That's lazy. And I don't get cookies if I don't.

- Teacher then asks class: "What did you notice from this conversation?" (Answers include "You paraphrased, asked for definition, asked for elaboration, etc.")
- Conversation line activity: Half the class lines up facing the other half of the class. When students are facing a partner, the teacher instructs students on the right side of the room to pose the prompt: "What is the lesson to be learned from reading this story? Should we act like the hen?" Instruct the left side to give a short answer so the right side can ask, "Can you explain that? Can you elaborate?" Then instruct the left side to pose the question to the right side, who will mumble their answer so the left side can ask, "Can you repeat that please? I didn't understand." Questions and prompts for clarify can be displayed on the CLARIFY anchor chart, on the board, in a slideshow, or on sentence strips. Then students in one line move over to a new partner, and they practice this skill again.

Review and Assessment

Teacher observes students and provides modeling and feedback to pairs. If something big goes right or wrong, the teacher can do an on-the-spot mini lesson.

Extension or Home-School Connection

Students have an academic conversation at home with a family member about a book they read. They practice clarifying.

Report back to class on how their conversations went.

ACTIVITIES FOR BUILDING THE SKILL OF CLARIFYING

- **Inside-Outside Circle (or Conversation Lines).** Half the students stand in a circle facing outward, the other half find a partner to face. Teacher provides a prompt, the inside circle answers in 20 seconds, and the outside circle paraphrases. Then they switch roles. Then the inside circle rotates. Repeat process for several turns.

- **Examples and Non-examples** (adapted from Beeman & Urow, 2012). Teacher shows a T-chart with examples of the concept on one side and non-examples on the other. This can be created electronically with each visual transitioning into the chart, or ideas can be on cards that students move to either side of the T-chart. After each visual example appears on the screen, students converse with a partner about the illustration and try to categorize the idea into one side.

- **Pair Plus One.** The third person is an observer who paraphrases during the conversation and provides feedback to the partners on the use of clarifying during the conversation. This observer can have "support cards" that he or she passes to either student when appropriate. A card might say, "Have your partner define the term." or "Paraphrase what your partner just said."

- **Assessing the Skill of Clarifying Ideas in Conversations**

You can formatively assess students' abilities to clarify relevant ideas by observing students and using the COAT; see Chapter 5). You can also use a basic checklist for assessing the skill:

- Do both students seem to be on the same page as they use key terms?

- Do they use clarifying moves to ask each other to clarify ideas?

- Do they try to be clear to partners (not just go through the motions)?

DEVELOPING CONVERSATION SKILL 3: SUPPORT AN IDEA WITH EXAMPLES, EVIDENCE, AND REASONS

In this sample conversation between two first graders, one student poses an idea, and the other student asks for elaboration. Then they continue to provide examples and question each other.

Armin: I think it's beaver's pond.

Delia: Why?

Armin: Cuz he made it to make his house.

Delia: But turtle is first in it.

Armin: So?

Delia: In the forest, out there, you find it first, and you have it. Same with the animals, I think.

Armin: But beaver made it a big pond bigger with the dam. So if he made it, he gets it. It's his, you know?

Delia: Maybe they need to share.

Armin: Do animals share?

Delia: Yeah. Like fish and frogs share water.

Armin: Yeah.

Once the idea is clarified as much as possible, it needs to be supported with evidence and reasoning. "Evidence" is another term used for specific information that supports an idea. Students in the primary grades must learn to use examples to strengthen ideas. For many students this is an introduction into more abstract and academic thinking that they will do throughout their lives.

During academic conversations, students may provide examples to clarify and to provide logical support for a perspective. For example, a student states that a character has changed from the start to the finish of the book. The partner could ask for examples to support that idea. In this case, the examples will all be directly from the text. However, there are four main types of examples that can be used during academic conversations.

1. **Examples from the text.** When students start with the text, they remind themselves to use the text as a model of academic language. Younger students also learn to refer to the text, as we see in the example of Armin and Delia above.

2. **Examples from other texts.** Younger students may have a limited repertoire of other texts to choose from. However, if the classroom teacher is instructing in thematic units, they can be encouraged to choose examples from texts the teacher has introduced. They can draw on examples from texts such as web pages, TV shows (if accurate), movies, and artwork.

3. **Examples from the world**. Accessing knowledge about the world can be challenging for younger learners. Teachers will need to train students to be continually observing and making links from the real world to the classroom. In the sample lesson plans provided, extension activities can include looking for examples in the real world.

4. **Examples from one's own life.** Using examples from one's own life is a common skill among primary grade students. Students often find it easier to share life examples, but this can sometimes take them off track. They need to be trained to think about whether the example is helpful or not to the overall conversation.

Younger students should be encouraged to think of examples in the order just given (1 through 4). It is much easier for them to jump straight to connecting to their own lives, but it is important to develop text evidence first and then move on to the personal connections as extra support. (See Figure 2.7.)

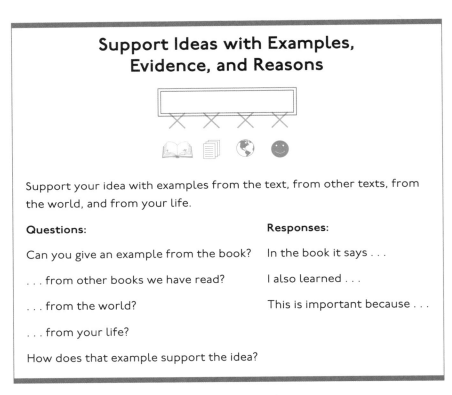

Figure 2.7   Anchor Chart for Support

 resources.corwin.com/ZwiersK3Guide

Sample Lesson Plan for Developing Academic Conversation Skills: Supporting With Examples, Evidence, and Reasons

This lesson includes similar routines as found in the lesson plans for the first two skills. We start with an introduction and multiple reviews of the SUPPORT anchor chart, gestures, and questions with responses. The teacher will teach key words, phrases, and target language structures for determining the central message or lesson. This SUPPORT lesson plan can be modified according to the grade level and language proficiency levels of the students.

Grade: First-Grade ELA/ELD

Standards Addressed

CCSS.ELA-LIT.RL.I.3, I.2: Describe characters and demonstrate an understanding of their central message or lesson.

CAL-ELD.PI.StrandII: Offer opinions and provide good reasons with detailed textual evidence or relevant background knowledge.

Objectives

Provide evidence that supports ideas for central messages during an academic conversation.

Performance Assessment

Paired conversations with the COAT.

Lesson Sequence

Introduce skill, build background, and create an idea

- Introduce language and content objectives.
- Build background—Show where China is on a map (Text: *The Empty Pot*).
- Teach the word "support".
- Teach gesture, icon, and questions and responses for "support." Refer to the SUPPORT anchor chart.
- "This week we will be practicing 'support an idea with examples.' After you create an idea and clarify it, you will need to provide examples to make your idea stronger. People may not believe your idea if you don't provide examples or evidence to back it up. There are four types of examples: examples from the text, from other texts, from the world, and from our lives. We will learn about each type of example."

- "We will read a story a couple of times and then try to figure out what the author is trying to teach through the story. As homework you will retell it to a family member when you go home this afternoon and describe the message using evidence from the story. Important details often include key characters and how they act or think, sometimes how they look, the main problem and minor problems that come up, and of course the final solution to the main problem."

- Read aloud and stop at times to have students summarize. Reread the story, if there is time.

- Fishbowl modeling: Teacher and student talk about prompt: "What is the author trying to teach us with this story?"

Student: First the emperor wants to find someone to take his place. So he decided to have a contest. Children had to grow seeds into flowers.

Teacher: Yes, and what do you think the message is for us, like how to be better people?

Student: I think not to lie.

Teacher: Interesting. What is evidence from the book that supports that?

Student: He doesn't use new seeds like the other kids. He brings the empty pot.

Teacher: That's good evidence. And he gets to be emperor because he was the only honest kid, right?

Student: Yeah.

Teacher: I think another message might be to keep trying.

Student: I agree.

Teacher: What can you ask me?

Student: Oh yeah. What's evidence of that?

- Teacher asks class: "What did you notice from this conversation?" (We each asked and gave evidence from the story to support ideas.)

- All students pair up and have academic conversations using the prompt with different stories they have read

Review and Assessment

Teacher observes conversations, looking for use of the skills: posing, clarifying, and especially supporting ideas.

Extension or Home-School Connection

Students have an academic conversation at home with a family member about a story they read. Try to come up with at least two messages or lessons from it.

ACTIVITIES FOR BUILDING THE SKILL OF
SUPPORTING IDEAS WITH EXAMPLES, EVIDENCE, AND REASONS

- **Examples & Non-examples** (adapted from Beck, McKeown, & Kucan, 2013). Teacher provides examples that support an idea mixed in with non-examples. Students are given a statement such as "Bats play an important role in nature." They are given cards with examples, reasons, non-examples, and nonrelated ideas. They need to choose which cards support the statement. For example, a card that says, "They eat tons of harmful insects every night" and "Some bats pollinate flowers of seeds and fruits that we eat" would support it, while "There are many species of bats" and "I love how bats can see in the dark" wouldn't support it.

- **Two or More Connected Sentences** (adapted from Zwiers, O'Hara, & Pritchard, 2014). Many students need to get into the habit of expressing their ideas with more than one sentence. This activity helps them start with two sentences. The first sentence will usually be the topic sentence, claim, or general statement. The second sentence (and others) will support the first sentence. Teacher modeling is key. For example, an English language learner (or any young student) may say, "About polar bears," for the main idea. Teachers should model how a main idea is crafted with a subject and verb and then how to find accurate examples to support the idea. "This text is about how polar bears live. For example, they need to swim a lot in cold water to go places."

- **Table Visual Organizer** (adapted from Zwiers & Soto, 2016). Similar to the visual in the anchor chart on page 38, students use a diagram of a table to show the skill of supporting an idea with evidence, examples, and logical reasoning.

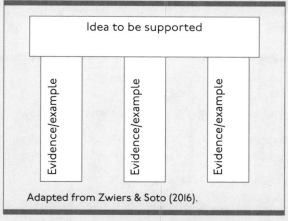

Table Visual Organizer

- **"Stronger & Clearer Each Time" Grids & Continuums** (adapted from Zwiers, O'Hara, & Pritchard, 2014). This set of activities is based on students having successive pair-shares in which they improve their ideas and language with each turn. It takes a little longer than a normal pair-share, but is often worth it with respect to content and language development. You can have students get into conversation lines or circles, which make the transitions less chaotic. In some cases, you can have them write their answers to your prompt before and after the activity to see the difference the pair-shares make. You can have students work on a wide range of interpersonal communication skills in addition to supporting, such as clarifying, nonverbal communication, validating the ideas of others.

  Have students meet with their first partners and tell them which line or circle talks first. Then use a sound (one ding) for turns to change in a partnership and another sound (two dings) for switching to another person. Notice positives and things to change during each pair-share, and in between the pair-shares you can emphasize and remind them to borrow ideas and language from partners to make their ideas stronger and clearer for the next partner. If you don't model this and remind them often, they will tend to just say the same thing or even less each time. You can also have students, when listening, to ask a support question to the partner (What's another example of that?), if desired. Remind students that one of their jobs is to help their fellow students talk more and talk more academically during the year.

  Opinion Continuum. If it is an opinion-based prompt, students can use a continuum and move their name along it (on a sticky note) depending on where they stand on the issue after each turn.

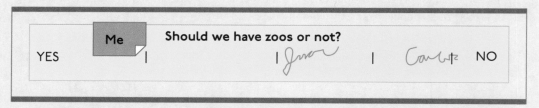

Sample Opinion Continuum

- **Assessing the Skill of Supporting Ideas in Conversations**

  You can formatively assess students' abilities to support ideas by observing students and using the COAT (see Chapter 5). You can also use a basic checklist for assessing the skill:

  ☐ Do both students provide evidence for the idea?

  ☐ Do they use questions to prompt their partners to provide examples, evidence, or reasons?

  ☐ Do they use academic terms in their responses? ("example," "reason," "evidence")

DEVELOPING CONVERSATION SKILL 4: EVALUATING-COMPARING-CHOOSING (ARGUING AND DECIDING)

Some conversations are argument-based, which means that students need to make a decision between two options or take a side in an argument. To do this they need to build up both ideas by clarifying and supporting them, ideally, one after the other. Many young children (and politicians) tend to limit their views to the first idea that comes to mind. Then they defend it like a super-hero before considering other points of view. However, life is full of multiple solutions and differing perspectives that our students must learn to address. They must learn to engage in "collaborative argumentation," which means that they work together to rationally and objectively look at all sides of an issue and make decisions.

After building up both (or multiple) ideas, students need to evaluate which one is stronger and choose it. This requires evaluation, a skill that, despite its abstract nature, primary grade students can and need to start developing. Figure 2.8 (below) is an anchor chart that can help you explain and model the skill.

Other skills that often support evaluating include: challenging the other person's evaluation of an idea ("I don't think that evidence is as strong as

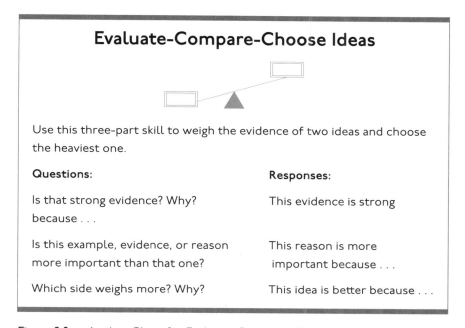

Use this three-part skill to weigh the evidence of two ideas and choose the heaviest one.

Questions:	Responses:
Is that strong evidence? Why? because . . .	This evidence is strong
Is this example, evidence, or reason more important than that one?	This reason is more important because . . .
Which side weighs more? Why?	This idea is better because . . .

Figure 2.8   Anchor Chart for Evaluate-Compare-Choose

you think it is") and negotiating ("So I guess we can say that sometimes it's OK to lie, like when . . ."). These subskills can be taught in separate mini lessons.

ACTIVITIES FOR BUILDING THE SKILL OF EVALUATING

- **Pro-Con.** In each pair there is a director and an actor. The teacher provides the prompt and a series of pictures or words that show the positive and negative aspects of an idea. For example, "Should we have a trampoline at school?" The director poses the question, claps hands, and says, "Pro!" The actor then says all the positive ideas, evidence, and reasons that he or she can, using the pictures as support. The director cuts the actor off at an appropriate time (to not let the partner use up all of his or her ideas) and says, "Con!," and the actor must then use an academic transition ("However," "On the other hand," Then again, etc.) to introduce the cons. They go back and forth a couple more times until the actor runs out of ideas.

- **Argument Balance Scale.** The balance scale is a visual (or manipulative) scaffold for getting students to build up both sides of a controversy or question and decide between two sides or options. Students decide which two sides are best to compare (school uniforms or not; dogs or cats are better pets; homework or not, etc.) and put them on each side. Then they work together to come up with reasons and examples that support

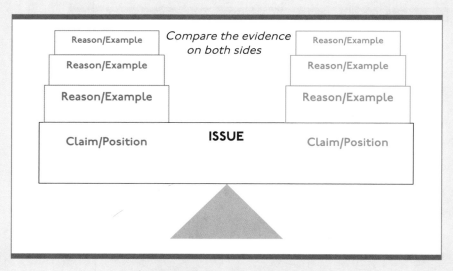

Argument Balance Scale Visual Organizer

(weigh down) each side. They should try to keep from telling their opinions right off and wait until they have filled in reasons and/or examples on each side. Then they compare sides to see which is heavier. You should model how to do this with a partner to maximize oral language used (e.g., you don't just want the more verbal or fluent kid filling in everything without any talk). You can model evaluation language such as "Which side weighs more? Why? Are any reasons bigger than other reasons? I think that this example is very strong because . . ."

- **"Stronger & Clearer Each Time" Opinion Continuum.** (See Stronger & Clearer Activity description on page 42.)

- **Highlight Academic Language.** Teach the comparative and superlative of *important*: "This evidence is important because . . ." "This example is more important than that example because . . ." "This reason is the most important because . . ."

- **Respectfully Disagree.** Ask students to pair up and each take a side of an issue. Tell them it doesn't matter if they don't truly believe their side; it is for the activity. The purpose is to learn to take different perspectives. For example pose the prompt, "Are cats better than dogs?" Then ask them to talk about the prompt while following these norms:

  o I respectfully listen to and try to understand others' ideas, even if I disagree.

  o I don't criticize or make fun of other students.

  o I value others, even if I challenge their ideas.

  o I know I am valuable, even if others disagree with my ideas.

  o I am open to changing my mind.

- **Assessing the Skill of Evaluating, Comparing, and Choosing Ideas in Conversations**

  You can formatively assess students' abilities to evaluate, compare, and choose relevant ideas by observing students and using the COAT (see Chapter 5). You can also use a basic checklist for assessing the skill:

  o Do both students seem to be on the same page as they negotiate the idea?

  o Do they use questioning moves to ask each other to compare ideas?

  o Do they decide on an idea that is supported by evidence and can they explain their thinking?

TIPS FOR DESIGNING CONVERSATION
PROMPTS ACROSS DISCIPLINES

Many teachers say how important it is to have a good prompt that sparks and drives a conversation. A good prompt is a bit like having good tinder and kindling to start a fire. It doesn't get going nor continue without it. Too many teachers think that a prompt is just a good open question, such as an essential question or question from the text. Yet the best prompts are more than just typical content questions. See what you notice about the following prompts.

Social Studies: With your partner, talk about why Rosa Parks is a hero and how we can be like her. Use ideas from the story that we read and the video that we saw. Make sure to clarify your ideas as much as possible. Use language such as "One heroic thing that she did was . . ."

Science: In pairs, have a conversation about why you think the moon appears to change shape from one night to the next. What could be happening? Make sure your explanations are clear and use scientific language such as "We believe that the moon appears to change shape because . . ."

Math: Work with your partner to create a word problem that requires the solver to add or subtract. Both of you take turns to share ideas for the problem and then you both decide which would make for the most interesting problem for your classmates to solve. Make sure the problem is very clear to others. You can include a drawing, too.

ELA Expository: Talk with your partner to decide if it is better to spend time watching television or reading books. Collaborate to build up both sides of the issue. For example, first talk about all the reasons and examples for watching TV. How is it helpful or good? Then do the same for reading books. Then decide which weighs more or has more or better evidence to support it. Use language such as "For example, evidence, this weighs more than that because . . ."

ELA Literature: Collaborate to come up with a lesson for the story. What do you think the author was trying to teach us readers with this story? Start by brainstorming several possible lessons and then decide on one. Find parts in the story that support that lesson and explain them. Use support language such as *support, evidence, because* . . . Also remember to use effective nonverbal communication.

Yes, these prompts are long. But their length helps guide and support the conversation. They make it clear what the goal of the conversation is (many students don't know why they are talking, even in high school).

You also likely noticed the three features of effective prompts introduced in Chapter 1. In each prompt,

1. **There is an engaging purpose** for conversing that (a) **connects to lesson objectives,** and (b) **requires thinking & doing something with ideas** (e.g., create, clarify, argue, come to a consensus, decide, rank, solve, evaluate, combine, compare, choose, fortify, build, and transform)

2. **There is a need to talk** (info gaps; bring unique ideas)

3. **There are clear directions** for how to converse (language use, thinking, content concepts . . .)

Sample Lesson Plan for Developing Academic Conversation Skills: Evaluating-Comparing-Choosing

In this lesson plan, notice the prompt is not addressing an academic subject. This is designed to provide the students with practice conversing about a familiar topic as the new skill is introduced. With this topic, most students will have background knowledge and vocabulary and thus be able to focus on practicing the new skill EVALUATE-COMPARE-CHOOSE. As usual, the teacher introduces the skill with a definition, gesture, and anchor chart. The language function provides an opinion and supports it with evidence. Another language function is to evaluate positives and negatives and negotiate a final agreement. How would you refine the objectives?

Grade: 2
Standards Addressed
• CCSS.ELA-LITERACY.RI.2.8-9: Describe how reasons support specific points the author makes in a text. Compare and contrast the most important points presented by two texts on the same topic.
• CA-ELD.PI.Strand3: Offer opinions and negotiate with others in conversations.
Objectives Collaborate with a partner to evaluate the evidence for ideas.
Performance Assessment Paired conversations on the questions. "Should we watch TV?" "What are positives and negatives of watching TV?"
Text Stories and articles with positives and negatives of watching TV.
Lesson Sequence *Introduce skill, build background, and create an idea* • Build background and interest: "Thumbs up or down if you think people should watch TV. That was a trick question. You all should have asked me for a lot of time to think about the thumbs up reasons and thumbs down reasons for watching

TV or not. Today we will take some time to look at both sides of a question and evaluate how heavy the reasons are on each side before we make a quick decision like many of you did just now."

- Teach the word "evaluate." "Does anyone recognize another word inside it?" Teach gesture, icon, and questions for "evaluate." Refer to the EVALUATE anchor chart.

- "This week we will be practicing 'evaluating ideas.' We learned how to create an idea, clarify it, and support it with examples. What happens if you and a partner or you and a group have more than one idea, and you need to choose the better one? You will need to evaluate the weight of the evidence for the ideas and decide which is the heaviest one. For example, your teacher might give you and your partner the chance to choose a book to read aloud to the class. You might want to read one book and your partner might choose a different book. How will you choose?"

- Read aloud anti-TV story, *Evil Tellies,* and pro-TV article

- Stronger & Clearer Each Time: Opinion Continuum: Model with teacher and a student. Introduce prompt: "Should we watch TV?" Yes and No on each side of the continuum. Students put a sticky note with their name on it where they stand on the issue. (Students can also move themselves in the room depending on where they stand on the issue.) Tell students they will talk with three partners, and each time what they say needs to be stronger and clearer. Listeners during the turn need to ask evaluation questions: Why do you think that is so important? Why does that evidence outweigh this evidence?

- Argument Balance Scale conversation—Prompt: "Should people watch TV or not?"

- Review objectives. Self-evaluation of evaluating ideas with rubric.

Extension or Home-School Connection

Students have an academic conversation at home with a family member: "Should we watch TV? If so, how much, which programs?" and so on.

Report back to class on answers.

CHAPTER SUMMARY

The four main academic conversation skills are prefaced by the cross-cutting skill of active listening. The sample anchor charts, lesson plans, and activities can be revised for implementing with students of different language proficiency and developmental levels. Embedded in the activities are opportunities for assessing student language and their abilities to implement the newly learned academic conversation skills during authentic conversations.

PLC PROMPTS FOCUSED ON TEACHING THE FIVE SKILLS

- When do young children use active listening skills outside of school?
- What icons, gestures, and sentence starters would work best for your students?
- How would you add to or adapt the sample anchor charts in this chapter?

ACADEMIC CONVERSATIONS FOR LITERACY

Academic reading and writing wither without rich conversations.

One of the main goals of primary classrooms is teaching students to read and write. There have been many heated debates about how to teach literacy. These debates tend to pit direct teaching of phonics versus indirect "whole language" strategies that focus on whole texts. Even though the pendulum still swings, most schools have settled on what is called a "balanced approach." And even the term "balanced" varies widely. What we tend to emphasize in this book is balancing the right strategies and text types for a given group of students. Students one year might need more phonics than the students needed the previous year, and so on. The key is to know what the different strategies are and how to match them with our current students.

The purpose of this chapter is to dig into the nitty gritty of how to build conversation skills and how to use conversations for developing students' literacy in primary grades. In most literacy programs there are conversations between students and between the teacher and students. What we do in this chapter is zoom in on ways to improve these conversations such that literacy thrives. We also look at how reading and writing can help students improve their conversation skills.

A MODEL FOR READING COMPREHENSION

Before looking at the model up close, it is important to reflect on what comprehension of text means, how it is assessed, and how it can differ among people. Robert Tierney (2009) describes it like this:

> It is a mistake to believe that there is some kind of precise "mathematic" or "formulaic" rendering that is possible. Meaning making is never precise; it is not a form of exact mapping of sounds or meanings onto text. Meaning making involves approximation or a form of allowable band of interpretations or elasticity to the meaning making between author or web-creator or film maker and reader and the world. (p. 262)

We can keep this idea in mind as we help students discuss text meanings in their conversations.

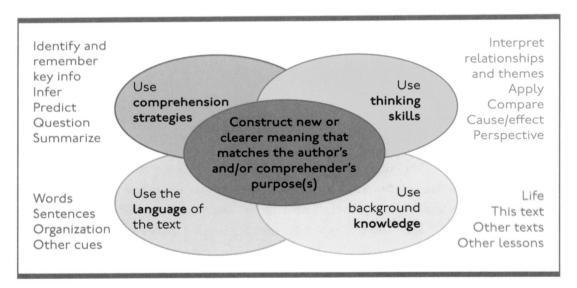

Figure 3.1   Reading Comprehension Model

As you can see, a lot happens inside a reader's mind to comprehend a written text, even in kindergarten. The central element in Figure 3.1 is the goal of comprehension: constructing new and clearer meaning that matches the author's and/or reader's purpose. In most cases, a reader first decodes the words and puts them together into phrases and sentences to construct initial rough drafts of meaning. As the listener or reader uses the text language, putting the words and sentences together, she also uses her background knowledge to visualize the meanings of words and sentences and connects to any other related knowledge. At the same time she keeps track of how well the meanings are matching the purposes for reading or listening. Additionally, the student uses both comprehension strategies such as predicting and questioning, as well as thinking skills such as interpretation and perspective, to further solidify and clarify the meaning of the message.

All five of these dimensions work together, with thoughts bouncing between them at lightning speed, to understand a text. When thoughts are happening in one of the outer four elements, it is important to consider how it supports the central element—and not linger too long on thoughts that don't support comprehension. For example, we have seen teachers spend too much time on vocabulary, at the expense of deep reading at the sentence and message levels.

COMPREHENSION CONVERSATIONS

Comprehension can and does happen in isolation, inside the mind of one person. Indeed, many of you right now are alone, comprehending the visuals and written words on these pages. But add a conversation with another person to this process, and you get a lot more comprehension and potential for language use. Another person comprehends differently and can offer new insights, questions, answers, descriptions, arguments, and so on. When two students talk about a text, they amplify its potential.

Here is the basic procedure for comprehension conversations, which are conversations that help students build their comprehension dimensions as they better understand a text.

1. Observe students to identify possible dimensions of comprehension that need extra work. For example, you might notice that several students aren't predicting or asking questions about the text. Other students might not connect to the previous similar texts that they had read. Choose a dimension to emphasize as they have conversations. (You could also have them use one prompt from each dimension.)

2. Read aloud a portion and then model, with a student as your partner, some questions from the focal dimension(s).

3. Have students pair up and read the text to one another or silently. You can also read to them on the carpet and have them pair up to answer questions when you stop.

4. Students respond to prompting from partners (e.g., "What do you think is going to happen? What do you think caused that to happen? Why? Why did the author write 'made his heart pound like a huge drum'? Is this like any previous story that we read?").

5. Remind students to show their listening and ask for clarification and supportive examples from the story. Remind them to make sure they don't go off on conversational rabbit trails and that they need to keep the central purpose in mind for why they are reading it and why the author wrote it.

6. If they are working just in pairs (you aren't reading aloud), they can stop and continue on their own. If you are reading aloud, wait until it quiets down a little, then read the next portion.

7. At the end of the text, have a whole class discussion that surfaces key aspects and questions and answers brought up in the paired discussions. You can use the large poster to write down a synthesis of what they comprehended in the center oval, and you can write down what they were supposed to understand from it and compare the two. (See Figure 3.2.)

Figure 3.2

Here is a first grade conversation halfway through a read aloud of *The Rainbow Fish*, a story in which the rainbow fish changes from being selfish and friendless to being generous and having friends. The students were trying to cover all four dimensions in the diagram. See which ones are which in the following conversation.

Alicia: I wanna know why he doesn't have friends.

Miguel: I think cuz he doesn't share.

Alicia: Share what?

Miguel: His color scales. That little fish wanted one, but the rainbow fish doesn't share.

Alicia: Oh. Yeah. I don't wanna be friends with him, too.

Miguel: I think he's gonna learn to share and get friends, maybe.

Alicia: Why?

Miguel: Cuz like the story yesterday. The dog learned to be nice. He changed. And this fish needs to change and be nice.

Alicia: Yeah. OK. What else?

Miguel: Language. Ask why he wrote something.

Alicia: Why did the fish say, "Who do you think you are?" to that little fish?

Miguel: I don't know. The little fish wanted a scale. Rainbow fish was mad at that. So maybe, to tell him he wasn't important.

Alicia: Yeah. What else?

Miguel: Connect to life. I like to eat fish.

Alicia: I think to share. We gotta share for friends; like we get friends if we share candy.

Notice in this conversation how the students used prompts from most of the dimensions and how it helped shape the conversation to build up comprehension. There are spots where each could have asked for and given more elaboration, but for first grade, this is an effective conversation.

FORTIFYING STUDENT READING
WITH ACADEMIC CONVERSATION SKILLS

Most of the things that you already do for reading can be beefed up with conversations and their skills to improve comprehension and overall learning of content. Here is a short list of popular approaches and some suggestions for strengthening them conversationally.

Readers' Workshop

A well-known approach for teaching reading is the workshop model (Calkins, 2010). First, the teacher provides explicit teaching in the lesson focus. Next, students engage in guided practice, either collaboratively or independently. Then, a significant period of time is devoted to independent work practicing the reading focus. During this independent time, teachers also meet with small groups of students or confer with readers. Collaborative academic conversations can fortify several areas within readers' workshop lessons.

Take a look at this sample conversation during a readers' workshop. The conversation is about an author study of Tomie dePaola in Grade 2. The two students are emerging bilinguals in a second-grade classroom.

Prompt: How did Tomie dePaola write in different genres? How are they different?

Enrique: What are autobiographies?

Shayleen: Um, *Boss for a Day*.

Enrique: Huh?

Shayleen: *Boss for a Day*.

Enrique: Yeah, you're almost close, but one of the books are *The Art Lesson* or *The Sister of Tommy*. So those are books that um . . . autobiography. Autobiography is that he's telling about his life.

Shayleen: What's fiction?

Enrique: A fiction book by Tomie dePaola is one that . . . *Strega Nona* because a pot can't, a pot can't, can't cook pasta on his own. Can you tell me a fiction book from Tomie dePaola?

Shayleen: I like a book of Tomie dePaola with *Boss for a Day*. Because um . . . because the girl. The dog, the girl tells the boy um . . . if . . . to um, he can boss for a day. Um, he can boss all day. She always boss him, and he doesn't do nothing.

Enrique: Can you tell me more?

Most published curricula include some suggestions and prompts for student-to-student interaction, such as whole class discussion, pair-shares and peer editing. However, few curricula offer extensive suggestions and scaffolds to help students be successful in paired conversations. The lesson below is an example of a teacher-created lesson in which the teacher models a conversation and refers to a chart with talk moves that students are supposed to learn.

Teachers have a responsibility to analyze their curricula and augment it with scaffolded opportunities for students to converse with each other. By integrating academic conversations and development of their skills throughout workshop-based instruction, teachers can provide even more punch to their instruction. For second language learners, student-to-student interaction provides a language-rich environment where students develop knowledge through dialogue.

This lesson from a first-grade readers' workshop curriculum illustrates how educators who write curriculum include authentic communication about books (see the "Guided Practice" and "Share" sections). However, the prompts can be refined to encourage in-depth academic conversations.

Here is a standards-based readers' workshop-focused lesson (Newton Public Schools, Newton, Massachusetts). Take a close look and notice its strengths. Also look through the lens of oral language and academic conversations, and notice where more conversation work could make it even stronger.

Lesson Focus	Retell stories, including key details, and demonstrate understanding of their central message or lesson. (CCSS. ELA-LITERACY.RL.1.2)
Connections *Activate prior knowledge. Explain how our work today is part of our ongoing unit of study.*	Yesterday we learned how readers find out who the main characters are in a book. Today we are going to focus on another important part of reading stories—the lessons or morals. Many authors like to teach readers how to be better people. Let's look at our literature toolkit and find the moral lesson and theme poster. Today we are going to learn how readers figure out what the author is trying to teach us with the story. It is important for readers to explain the moral lesson when they are talking about their books, so listeners can get an idea of how the story can help us become better people.

(Continued)

(Continued)

Modeling *Teach something students will try in their reading*	Here is a story that we read last week. Can someone retell it quickly? I will help. Now what do you think we were supposed to learn from this story? How should we act? What should we say? (Whole class) I think the theme was to be nice to people, even if they aren't nice to us. Do you agree?
Guided Practice *Students practice the strategy with support: then turn and talk with partners; or try out alone*	Now I'm going to read several pages of the book we are currently reading. I want you to follow along as I read them and think about the possible themes or lessons that the author might try to teach us. Do you have any ideas? It's OK to have different ideas. Okay, now I want you to turn to your partner and tell him or her what you think the lesson might be. Use information from the story and from previous stories or your life. For example, if you think the lesson is to work hard to reach your goals, then say, "For example, in the story Juan kept on trying to get better at hockey. He even stayed up all night one time practicing his shot."
Work Time	Use a sticky note to write down what you think the strongest theme is so far.
Share	Did you pay attention to the characters and setting as you read today? Can I have a few volunteers share character names and the setting from their book?

So how could this lesson be modified to help students *go beyond* the standards? By providing a solid prompt and some modeling of how to start and extend a conversation, the teacher could encourage a stronger conversation. Consider the engagement and helpfulness of this prompt, "Now I want you to turn to your partner and ask, 'What do you think a strong theme was?' If you need elaboration or support, ask, 'Why do you think that?'" By modeling this conversation first, the teacher will show how each partner has a chance to ask and answer the question. The teacher could also use the anchor chart in Figure 3.3.

The "Share" step can also be revised to ask, "Can I have a volunteer to share what your partner told you about his or their idea?" By inquiring about the partner's idea, the teacher is reaffirming the expectation that partners listen carefully to each other. Students are held accountable for listening and processing another person's talk. The teacher is able to assess whether or not students are approaching standards (e.g., SL 1.3) and truly asking each other about the texts and clarifying information when necessary. The reflection step incorporates both content and language development. Teachers also use

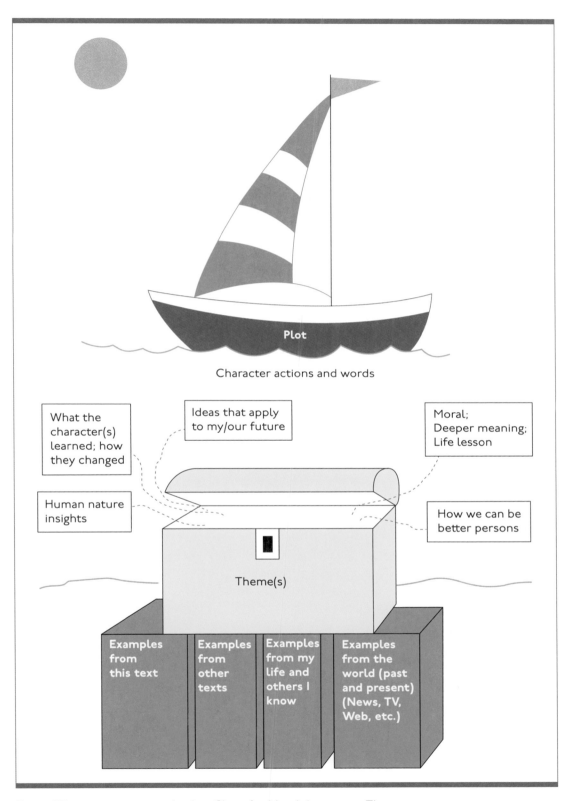

Plot

Character actions and words

What the character(s) learned; how they changed

Ideas that apply to my/our future

Moral; Deeper meaning; Life lesson

Human nature insights

How we can be better persons

Theme(s)

Examples from this text

Examples from other texts

Examples from my life and others I know

Examples from the world (past and present) (News, TV, Web, etc.)

Figure 3.3   Anchor Chart for Moral, Lesson, or Theme

this time to focus the discussion on students' metacognition about progress (Moses, 2015). Often teachers "run out of time" and skip this important step.

AUGMENTING READ ALOUDS

A read aloud is an opportunity for the teacher to share books that are slightly challenging, culturally relevant, and engaging for students. By pausing during the read aloud to pose conversation prompts, students can practice comprehension thinking, articulate their thoughts with others, and build up ideas together. See page 61 for an anchor chart that can help prompt rich discussions.

The most common classroom configuration for a read aloud in primary grades is having students sit together on the rug. Ask students to sit next to a conversation partner who can provide linguistic support. Charts with key phrases can be available and conversations should be briefly modeled, especially early in the school year when students are becoming familiar with the core communication skills.

Read alouds depend on and build stamina in the use of listening skills. Students must listen to the text being read aloud and be ready to answer prompts along with others. They must listen for the gist and key details for use as evidence when they have their conversations. This is a challenge for primary students, as you know. You can scaffold these skills by modeling a conversation, providing conversation starters, (See Figure 3.4 below) pre-teaching target vocabulary, and using picture cues or manipulatives.

Genre	Conversation Starters
Fiction/poetry	How does the main character feel? Why? How is the main character changing? What is this story or poem trying to teach us?
Nonfiction	What was the most important information you have learned? Why is it important?
Argument	Do you agree with the author? Why? Why not? Has the author built up both sides of the argument?
Biography/ autobiography	Why did this person write about her, his, or this life? What was the most important trait or deed of this character? What would you like to write about in your autobiography in 30 years?

Figure 3.4   Conversation Starters During and After Read Alouds, by Genre

Challenge students to increase the quantity and quality of turns. You can tell students to take at least four turns apiece to answer the prompt. You can time the turns and tell them to try to fill the 30 seconds (or other amount of time) for each turn by clarifying and using examples from the text.

ROLE-BASED IMPROV CONVERSATIONS

In many stories and even nonfiction texts, there are multiple characters with different perspectives. This activity allows students to take on different roles and describe the perspectives of the person or character whom they embody. It allows many students who are shy about sharing their own ideas and perspectives to have a creative way to express themselves and verbalize ideas. Sometimes, there can be less "risk" (and therefore more language produced) when sharing from someone else's perspective than one's own. And it can be fun.

1. Pick a text that has characters with different things to share with one another (different perspectives, opinions, stories, motivations, etc.).

2. Tell students the prompt (e.g., "You will converse with your partner about which one of your brothers was more right. You will come to an agreement").

3. Assign roles for each pair (e.g., younger brother and older brother).

4. Have students read the text with the prompt in mind, taking notes on what they will say, based on their role.

5. Have them review their notes and put them onto one note card, with key words and not in complete sentences.

6. Have students converse with their roles in mind (using conversation skills, etc.).

FORTIFYING STUDENT WRITING WITH ACADEMIC CONVERSATION SKILLS

For workshops and other approaches to the teaching of writing, academic conversations can provide students with practice using language orally before transferring it to writing. Primary students, in particular, can benefit from talking before, during, and after writing—even when their writing is not completely decipherable. When they talk before writing, they practice the language they might use in their compositions, and they hear new language from others that they can use. During writing, as in the drafting, editing, and revising stages, conversations allow students to reflect on the clarity of language in a piece of writing, especially as others read their words and provide feedback. And after writing, conversations allow students to further process the ideas and to orally use the more formal and academic language(s) used to describe the ideas recently written down.

All approaches and strategies for teaching writing can be augmented with conversations in some way. Here are few ideas.

Writers' Workshop

A well-known approach for developing writing skills in primary grades is writers' workshop. These workshops provide a great platform for building conversation skills—and conversation skills can be very effective at improving the workshops and students' writing! Students often work in pairs to brainstorm and elaborate ideas for writing, help their peers improve drafts, and respond to final drafts during writing celebrations. Teachers should model and support conversations and their skills at stages of the writing process.

In writers' workshop conversations, prompts need to be carefully crafted to elicit original ideas, use target vocabulary, and experiment with new language structures. Teachers scaffold these academic conversations by modeling the language, offering response starters, and providing word banks. The following table can help.

Stage	How to fortify it conversationally
1. Brainstorm topics and choose one to write about.	Have both students take turns prompting one another for ideas. Then they look at each one and talk about which is better to write about and why. Talk about any similar texts that they have read that might be models for what they will write.
2. Gather and organize ideas (read, research, use graphic organizers, etc.).	They talk about how they will organize (semantic map, story map) details and the order to put them in.
3. Write first draft.	They talk about each sentence and decide if it is complete and clear enough. They remind each other to put in punctuation and take turns reading the draft to one another.
4. Revise (with the feedback of teacher, peers, others) to organize, add, or subtract ideas to make it stronger and clearer.	They meet with another pair who reads their draft, talks about the positives and possible suggestions to make it clearer and stronger (e.g., use more details, use juicy words). The new pair shares their ideas about possible changes to make, and the pair talks about the feedback to make changes if they think they will help.

Stage	How to fortify it conversationally
5. Edit for grammar and punctuation.	Both students read the piece again to one another and talk about where and if punctuation or grammar changes are needed. If it sounds weird, it likely could be clarified.
6. Write final draft and publish.	Students work together to write the final draft, asking each other along the way if a part is clear and if any final changes might help.

Here is a transcript from two third-grade students in a sheltered English classroom having a conversation about character changes at the first stage of writers' workshop. The writing prompt is "Describe a character in a story who changes from the beginning to the end." The graphic organizer they completed before the discussion had four rows to take notes about characters from four different texts. The graphic organizer had two columns: one for the beginning of the story and one for notes from the end of the story.

Elena: Do you know any story that has character changes?

Daniela: Yes, *The Ugly Vegetables*.

Elena: What happened before?

Daniela: She was feeling embarrassed.

Elena: Um hum. What happened after?

Daniela: She was proud of herself.

Elena: Do you know any other stories?

Daniela: "James Ale."

Elena: What happened before?

Daniela: James Ale was feeling embarrassed because a car hit Bobby.

Elena: Uh huh. What happened after?

Daniela: He feels proud because he made a park.

Elena: Can you please say that one more time? I didn't understand what you said.

Daniela: What part? *(Pointing to paper.)* After. He feels proud because he made a park for kids to go play there.

Elena: *(Smiles and nods.)* So I know *Muggie Maggie*. Before, Maggie did not know cursive.

Daniela: Ummm . . .

Elena: After, she learned cursive.

Daniela: *(Nods.)*

Elena: Do you know any other stories?

Daniela: Do you know another story?

Elena: *The Ugly Vegetables.*

Daniela: *(Nods.)*

Elena: Before the girl was embarrassed. After, she liked more vegetables to do soup and eat.

Daniela: OK.

Elena: I liked talking about the character changes.

Daniela: Me, too. I liked talking to you because I liked how you did complete sentences.

Elena: I like that we did eye contact. And also we did "um hum." *(Nods head.)*

What strengths do you notice about the conversation between these two students? What were they able to do language-wise (vocabulary, sentences,

Students should converse before, during, and after writing.

organization)? How did they use core conversation skills to keep their conversation going? How can this conversation help their writing? If you were their teacher, what lessons would you design to help them move forward in their conversation skills and linguistic complexity to improve their writing? And there are more juicy questions like these. These questions show both the power and complexity of conversation work, even in primary grades.

Describe and Narrate Info Gap

In this activity, each student in an A-B pair reads different texts or looks at different visual resources. For example, you would give all *A*s in a pair the same two pictures or texts, and you would give *B*s two different pictures or texts.

In the first stage, the student takes some time to look at and summarize, explain, or describe each resource. For example, you might give each student a picture of different animals that might interact with each other in an ecosystem. Each student practices, orally, describing to the partner the physical characteristics of the animal, any features that help it survive, and the image's background. Then they write their descriptions down (if they can write). Next, each student looks at his or her second picture, which might be of an additional animal or of an event that happens in the setting of the pictures. Then in Stage 2, the students work together to create a story that connects all the pictures (or texts) together. They can then meet with another pair and create a group story that combines the ideas from each pair. Here is an excerpt from a second-grade Describe and Narrate Info Gap conversation about pictures of sheep, a sheep dog, a fox, and a shovel.

Alma: OK, now the story. What happens?

Samuel: I think this fox tries to get sheep.

Alma: Yeah. Good. And the dog comes and scares the fox, maybe *ladra* (barks). Write it.

Samuel: OK. The end? What about the *pala* (shovel)?

Alma: No. Maybe the fox comes back again. And the dog gets tired of scaring him every, every night.

Samuel: So he makes a hole *para atrapar el zorro* (to trap the fox).

Alma: Yeah. Good. And the fox falls in it.

Samuel: And all sheep laugh of him.

Graphic Organizers

Graphic organizers are used for a variety of purposes in school, a big one being to organize ideas for writing. Often students are simply given the organizer and told to fill it in. Yet in doing so, teachers miss out on rich opportunities for conversation based on the organizer. We describe the conversational use of just three organizers here. Other examples are Venn diagrams, charts, graphs, flowcharts, and diagrams. As you read this section, think about the many visuals that you use and think about how they can be used to foster and extend conversations between students. (And share your ideas with us!)

Story Map. Have students meet to talk about their individual story maps or to create a joint story map. Model the use of language that students can use, such as "What is the main problem or challenge of the story?" "How does the main character solve the problem?" "What is the main lesson that we learn to be better people?" "Who are the characters? Why them? What should happen first, second, third, and so on? How can the main character change?" You can also structure their interactions so that one student doesn't dominate with either the questions or the answers.

Semantic Map. Semantic maps tend to be used for nonfiction ideas and relationships. For example, students might be learning about a certain animal, which they would put in the center of the map and put things like habitat, food, appearance, and behaviors on the outside. Or in studying astronauts, they might put "living in space" in the center, and food, work, communication, and health on the outside. Then branching out from each of these categories would be details related to each one. Students, in conversation, can work together to decide the categories and then where the details go. They can also decide if a detail is important enough to write down (or draw) on the map.

Argument Balance Scale. (See description in Chapter 2). You can use Argument Balance Scale conversations to prepare students for writing arguments.

CHAPTER SUMMARY

This chapter offers a model for text comprehension. We also discuss implications for conversations in readers' and writers' workshops. Traditionally, the workshop method has focused on building independent reading and writing skills. By adding a conversation with another person to the workshop model, you get a lot more comprehension and potential for language use. Through the process of creating and clarifying ideas, partners can offer new insights, questions, answers, descriptions, arguments, and so on. When two students talk about a text, they bring their background knowledge to the conversations and learn from each other in the process.

PLC PROMPTS FOCUSED ON LITERACY

- How is building stamina in speaking and listening similar to building stamina in reading and writing? How is it different?

- How do you describe the connection between conversing and reading? How about conversing and writing?

- Complete the Conversation Observation and Analysis Tool (COAT; see Chapter 5) for the conversation about Tomie dePaola or character changes. Compare your responses to your colleagues. What did you notice about language use? How would you adjust instruction to promote language acquisition?

- Which activities in our curriculum can we revise to promote academic conversations during reading or writing instruction?

CHAPTER 4

ACADEMIC CONVERSATIONS IN SCIENCE, SOCIAL STUDIES, MATH, AND ART

Each child's mind is a beautiful forest.

The power of building academic conversation skills is multiplied when conversations happen across disciplines. When students practice the skills and target language throughout the school day, they learn content, language, and social skills that last. A conversation between two scientists will tend to be very different from a conversation between two historians or a conversation between two mathematicians. We want students, even in primary grades, to begin to build habits for engaging in these different types of conversations.

The conversation work in this chapter builds on the information presented in the previous chapters. Conversations in this chapter depend on the five core skills presented in Chapters 1 and 2, and we refer to activities described in Chapter 3. Of course, the reason for writing this chapter is to describe ways in which conversations in different disciplines are different and to give examples that will help you maximize the support you can give students as they talk about a wide range of disciplinary topics.

iStock.com/asiseeit

Conversation helps to clarify content.

ACADEMIC CONVERSATIONS IN SCIENCE

Within the four main domains of science taught in school (physical, life, Earth and space, and engineering design), there are many opportunities for academic conversations. For example, the Next Generation Science Standards ask students to develop in-depth understanding of content while they practice key skills including communication, collaboration, inquiry, problem solving, and flexibility. Not by coincidence, conversations do these things very well.

Integrated throughout the standards are "cross-cutting science concepts and skills" such as interpreting data and identifying causes and effects in scientific phenomena. These cross-cutting concepts also stand out as key leverage points for language development. When teaching language through and for science, teachers can provide scaffolds for students to incorporate certain types of language into their conversations. To successfully support these conversations, it's important to think about the design of the prompt, the language that you want students to use, any visual scaffolds that your students might need, and the ways in which you will help them build up a critical mass of content knowledge to use in the conversations. As the old saying goes, "Juicy conversations don't grow on trees." It's a relatively new old saying.

While there are a great many types of conversations that primary students can have about science topics, we emphasize three types of conversations here. These are (1) deciding between two sides of a controversial science issue, (2) collaborating to interpret data and explain causes and effects of scientific phenomena, and (3) role-based improv conversations. We provide a description of each, with sample conversations.

Science Type I: Deciding Between Two Sides of a Controversial Science Issue

While some of these topics might arise in language arts lessons, it also helps to have students argue in science lessons about solutions to problems and controversial topics that arise. Students can learn about (through read-alouds, reading, video, or images) a current dilemma or problem that requires science thinking and talking to resolve.

Of course, you will usually need to model with a student how to build up both sides of the issue with evidence and reasoning. Helpful scaffolding for this type of conversation includes the visual organizers (e.g., balance scale) and sentence frames such as "Let's first build up one side of the issue. What examples support this side? Which side is stronger/heavier?" Here is a sample conversation in second grade about cutting down trees.

Paty: Let's build up one side of the issue.

Ana: One side is to cut them is OK.

Paty: I think that's bad.

Ana: Me, too, but we gotta build it up anyway.

Paty: OK. What examples support it?

Ana: They need wood for houses. What do you have?

Paty: They need to make fences. And some people make tables and chairs.

Ana: That's enough. The other side, now.

Paty: Trees are alive. We shouldn't kill them.

Ana: And lots of things live in them. Like monkeys and birds.

Paty: So they die if the trees are cut down, right?

Ana: Yeah. It's bad.

Paty: Me, too.

Notice in this conversation how the students used the structure of supporting one idea first, even though they didn't agree with it, and then they moved on to the other idea. Notice the language of examples and support in this conversation.

Right now, think about the topics and lessons that you teach in science and brainstorm possible conversation prompts that ask students to interpret and come up with explanations for scientific phenomena. Here are some prompt examples:

- Why does the moon look different each night?

- What do plants do or have to help them survive?

- What happens when materials vibrate?

- How do plant seeds get spread around?

- How can we find out the best amounts of sun and water needed by a plant?

- Why are the days longer in summer than in winter?

Science Type 2: Collaborating to Interpret Data and Generate Scientific Explanations

Science Type 2 is the most common type of conversation in science, because it covers many of the science standards for primary grades. Even though they are young, primary students need to get a solid start in interpreting scientific observations and "data" as well as crafting explanations for phenomena. They can look at what they have observed and think about what kinds of scientific explanations they can come up with. For example, students can observe animals at a zoo or aquarium (or in a picture) and count the number of different animals to make a bar graph. They can then interpret and explain why there are large or small numbers of animals in the ecosystem or how certain features help animals to survive and so on. They might touch a vibrating guitar string and put together a more general explanation that connects vibration to sound production.

It helps to model with a student how to come up with a wide range of different types of interpretations and speculations: Helpful scaffolding for this type of conversation includes the visual organizer and sentence frames such as "I see in the bar graph that there are more . . . I think this means that . . ." Here is a sample conversation. The teacher had them start with "What do you think about what you see?" and "What does that mean?"

Emilio: What do you think?

Rahel: I see in my graph more small fish than sharks. Only one shark.

Emilio: So what does that mean?

Rahel: It means maybe sharks eat the fish?

Emilio: So maybe there got to be lots of fish.

Rahel: Why?

Emilio: Cuz too many sharks eat up everything. Then they die when it's all gone.

Rahel: I agree. What do you think?

Emilio: I see the crabs got pinchers. I think they help them grab food.

Rahel: And to fight sharks, maybe, too?

Emilio: Yeah. I want to see that.

Notice in this conversation how the students used the scaffolds and covered two different kinds of observations, one about numbers and one about features of animals that help them survive. Notice the language use at the word, sentence, and message levels. At the word level, the students use the term "graph" so we can tell they are observing data. At the sentence level, they pose questions that are grammatically correct. We notice the use of the verb "got" instead of "have." At the message level, the students stay on topic. They also use communication skills such as asking, "What do you think?" The final line by Rahel is an indication that she is visualizing the animals in the ocean, indicating that the conversation is helping her immerse (no pun intended) herself in the content that she is learning.

Right now, think about the topics and lessons that you teach in science and brainstorm possible conversation prompts that ask students to interpret and come up with explanations for scientific phenomena. Here are some prompt examples:

- Why does the moon look different each night?
- What do plants do or have to help them survive?
- What happens when materials vibrate?
- How do plant seeds get spread around?

- How can we find out the best amounts of sun and water needed by a plant?

- Why are the days longer in summer than in winter?

Science Type 3: Role-Based Improv Conversations

This type of conversation allows students to be a little more creative and dramatic, while supporting the learning of science and its language (see the general description of role-based improv conversations in Chapter 3). Students take on the role of two different things or processes and have a conversation in those roles. For example, a glacier might talk to a river, an ocean to a lake, a mammal to a reptile, one planet to another, volcano and earthquake, sun and moon, snake and eagle, dinosaur and rat, a city to a farm.

Of course, a hefty amount of modeling and preparation is usually required for extended conversations between students. Helpful scaffolding for this type of conversation can include visual organizers that remind students of the types of science content they should talk about in their roles. Sentence frames can also help: "I think we are different in several ways. For example, you . . . and I . . . We seem to have some things in common, like . . ." Here is a sample conversation. The teacher had them start with "Tell me about yourself. What do you do?" and then move to "How are we different and similar?"

José: Tell me about yourself. What do you do?

Napreet: I am the planet Earth. I have lots of water on me and some land. That's where people live. And animals. And I'm round.

José: Animals live in water, too, right? Like fish and whales.

Napreet: Yeah.

José: So what do you do?

Napreet: I spin. And I go around the sun.

José: The sun goes around you.

Napreet: No. I spin so it looks like it.

José: I don't agree.

Napreet: OK. Tell me about yourself. What do you do?

José: I'm the moon. I don't have no air, and I got lots of craters.

Napreet: What's craters?

José: Big round holes. I think from bombs, maybe.

Napreet: So what do you do?

José: I go around Earth, you. And I change, like light on me.

Napreet: OK, so how we similar?

José: We're round and we move.

Napreet: And how are we different?

José: I don't have water but you do; and nobody lives on me, I don't think.

Notice the engaging nature of playing roles and the many turns that were facilitated by the structure. Also notice the content being discussed—and that they had been well prepared to share different features of each thing. Notice the language questioning, describing, personifying, and clarifying. Take a moment to think about two different things in your science unit that could "have a conversation."

Sample Academic Conversation Lesson Plan for Science

Here is a lesson plan with some Type 3 conversations. In this lesson, students are asked to understand and compare various features of plants. They hold and observe grass and a pumpkin and then make interpretations, comparisons, and explanations.

Grade: Kindergarten

Standards Addressed

- K-LSI-I: Use observations to describe patterns of what plants and animals (including humans) need to survive.
- ELA/Literacy—W.K.7: Participate in shared research and writing projects (e.g., explore a number of books by a favorite author and express opinions about them). (K-LSI-I)
- K.MD.A.2: Directly compare two objects with a measurable attribute in common, to see which object has "more of" or "less of" the attribute and describe the difference. (K-LSI-I)

Objectives

- Distinguish between the parts of the plant and name them.
- Explain what each part of the plant does as its function.
- Compare grass and pumpkins.

Performance Assessment

- Label parts of a plant for a brochure.
- Converse with a partner about the similarities and differences between grass and pumpkins.

Lesson Sequence

Introduce skill, build background, and create an idea

- Introduce language and content objectives.
- Build background—Ask students to name plants and ask what they know about plants (Texts: *From Seed to Plant* by Gail Gibbons; *Seed, Sprout, Pumpkin Pie*—National Geographic).
- Review parts of the plant.
- Review compare and contrast language: "similar," "different," "both."

- Pass around the grass and a small pumpkin.

- Fishbowl modeling: Teacher and student introduce prompt: "How are grass and pumpkins similar and different?"

Student:	How are grass and pumpkins similar?
Teacher:	The grass has a long stem. The pumpkin also grows on a stem that is thick and grows close to the ground.
Student:	So you are saying they both have stems. *(Shows a colored counter to indicate that he has successfully paraphrased.)*
Teacher:	Yes. And how are they different?
Student:	The pumpkins have yellow flowers. Grass does not have flowers.
Teacher:	So you are saying that pumpkins have flowers. On the other hand, grass doesn't have flowers? Why do you think they have flowers?
Student:	For bees to go to?
Teacher:	Yeah, I think bees like pretty flowers, and they spread pollen around.
Teacher asks class:	What did you notice from this conversation?

- Students pair up for conversations. They have access to labeled photos of the parts of the plants and a chart with signal terms for making comparisons.

Review and Assessment

Teacher reviews numbers of conversation counters that students have employed during their conversations.

Extension or Home-School Connection

Students have an academic conversation at home with a family member: What plant can you see in our home or neighborhood? What are the parts? Report back to class on answers.

The teacher provided visual supports with labeled photos of the parts of the plant. The prompt was "How are pumpkins and grass similar and different?" The language function in the lesson is "compare and contrast." Language for comparing was taught directly, in addition to the content-specific plant terms. Pay careful attention to the conversation and look for ways in which these kindergarten students use conversation skills to extend and deepen the conversation. Also consider the helpfulness of the turn-taking support.

Arax: Grass is different from pumpkins. Grass has little seeds, a pumpkin seeds is little bigger.

Frances: Bigger or medium? *(Gestures.)*

Arax: Medium. Your turn.

Frances: Grass is bigger, but pumpkins are circle. They both, they are different. *(Flips counters.)*

Arax: Pumpkin and grass is not different because pumpkins has um . . .

Frances: Maybe seeds inside. Maybe seeds inside.

Arax: Pumpkin is bigger um . . . bigger . . . bigger . . . grass is little smaller.

Frances: *(Gestures.)* Um . . . pumpkin has seed inside but grass doesn't have any seed inside.

Arax: Um . . .

Frances: Do you want me to go again?

Arax: Pumpkin and grass have the same as grass and grass has flowers and pumpkins has too flowers.

Frances: Pumpkins are have um . . . stems but grass doesn't have stems. So because if a pumpkin doesn't have stems that if they have stems that's why they get bigger, but the grass doesn't have stems so that's why they are little.

Students use language for comparing and contrasting ("same," "different from," "both," "bigger," and "smaller.") We also notice more complex sentences: "Pumpkin has seed inside but grass doesn't have any seed inside." Conversation skill-wise, the first question posed was to clarify: "Bigger or medium?" The second question ("Do you want me to go again?") is a great example of how Frances was able to move the conversation forward, helping out Arax, who was temporarily stuck. And at the end Frances interprets and explains the reason why pumpkins are large: because they have stems and grass doesn't.

This conversation provides rich data for the teacher who can think carefully about any scientific misconceptions students have. For example, the teacher might clarify that grass does have stems. Another next step for teaching is to explain the use of "a little bit" as a modifier of "bigger" and "smaller." We can also have them practice the terms "both" and "similar." At the discourse level, the students would benefit from practicing how to end a conversation. Instead of "We are finished," they could say, "We agree that grass and pumpkins are similar because they both need water and sun. And they are different because the pumpkin is round and orange."

Analyze a Sample Conversation from Third Grade

In contrast to the kindergarten conversation in science, try analyzing an example of a third-grade conversation in science. In this conversation about the life cycle of plants, two third-grade English learners use text features (including comprehension questions and diagrams) as support for their ideas. The conversation was in their English language development class, but they drew on their background knowledge from the study of ecosystems learned during science. The language focus was sequencing, and there were some support questions to help students extend their conversations.

Kiarelys: What is the most interesting fact you learned about plants?

Ricardo: I learned that the life cycle is when they grow, they plant the seed, it's growing the, um, the . . . *(Looks back in book, finds diagram of life cycle and points at illustrations.)* Open the seed, then the stem, and then the leaf grow, and then the flowers open to the food, and then the fruit and then the seed comes and they grow another band of those, they grow and they grow and they grow, and that is the life cycle.

Kiarelys: You said first the seed, and then the stem, and the root. And then the fruit and then the seed comes out and then they grow again and again.

Ricardo: So conclusion. How does stems and roots help the plant grow?

Kiarelys: They have the stems hold the water and the roots grow for the flowers can grow more.

Ricardo: I understand you. Can you tell me more?

Kiarelys: And . . . and they um . . . grow in the soil.

Ricardo: I understand you. You said the plants grow and then the water came and then the root. You said the root hold the water and then pass it to the plant and then to the soil. They save it in the soil and then when they are tired, they get some.

Kiarelys: Explain the life cycle of a plant.

Ricardo: The, the, the life cycle of a plant is the . . . it help the like um . . . they're passing water. They're like helping each other. Put the seed and grow and grow up. *(Gestures.)* It come bigger and then the bird comes and she bites her. And then when she all tired she . . . (nods abruptly) and then grow the seed and then she open the couch. Like, you know, the cover. *(Gestures.)*

Kiarelys: Oh, you said that they help each other. They pass the water. They grow. The bug come and eat the honey.

Ricardo: It grow, like the plant of a bean. Then it open and the bean gets into the um . . . and then it comes another flower and that's how the life cycle.

Kiarelys: Why do you think most people like plants?

Ricardo: The . . . because they're beautiful and they give food to the people and they give energy to the people like the food and the beans and the tomatoes and all those and that's why the people like flowers.

Kiarelys: I understand that you say that people like because they are beautiful, the flowers. And they give us many food from the flowers.

Ricardo: And that helps us. And that's all.

In this beautifully long conversation, we notice strong ideas on the part of both students but that they could have used a better variety of transition phrases for describing sequences. The common sequence word used is "then." This could be an area to focus future instruction. The teacher could directly teach students to incorporate words and phrases like "after," "next," "at first," and "finally." Targeted instruction in sequencing across a range of topics, along with continued oral practice, will likely help them be clearer when it comes to sequences.

In addition, at the discourse level of analysis, these two students also struggle with how to end the conversation. They look up and then Ricardo states, "And that's all." How would you want these students to end their conversation? In this case, the teacher might model how to conclude the conversation with a final summary that focuses on the life cycle and not on why people like plants. This could train students to go back to the original prompt and think about what science and language they were supposed to work on.

ACTIVITIES FOR BUILDING THE SKILL OF ACADEMIC CONVERSATIONS IN SCIENCE

- **Written Conversations.** In written conversations students have one piece of paper and respond to one another in writing in succession. You can prompt for any of the three types of science conversations described on pages 73–77. You then have a helpful record of their thinking and their conversation skills that you can analyze to inform future teaching.

- **Role-Based Improv Conversation** between two things. See the example on page 76 of a Type 3 conversation (role-based).

- **Co-Design an Experiment.** Students can read a science text or observe a phenomenon and converse to design an experiment to go with it or answer a question. For example, after reading a book about plants, students can ask, "How do scientists learn about plants? What can we do to learn more? What tools and materials do we need? What questions will we ask?"

- **Examples and Non-examples.** See description on page 36.

- **Model and Scaffold Key Thinking Skills Terms for Science.** You can use this poster, or something similar, to help students use science language in their conversations and other activities.

Core Skills and Terms Used in Thinking in Science	Sample Questions	Sample Responses
Hypothesize predict, think, guess	What do you think will happen? What do you predict?	I think that . . . I predict . . .
Design experiments prove, plan, observe, test, if . . . then . . .	How could we prove this? What can we observe?	We need to plan . . . I observe . . .

(Continued)

(Continued)

Core Skills and Terms Used in Thinking in Science	Sample Questions	Sample Responses
Cause and effect because, as a result, one reason, another reason	What were some causes? What is the result?	The causes were . . . Some reasons were . . .
Sequence first, second, third, then, next, finally	What happened first? Is there a cycle?	First . . . Then . . . Next . . . The cycle is . . .
Observe patterns if . . . then . . . , always, sometimes, never, as you can see	What did you notice? What did you wonder?	They both . . . I wonder why . . .
Evaluate change in conclusion, therefore	What happened? What is the main result?	This is important because . . . As a result . . .
Compare both, alike, however, one difference, on the other hand	What are the similarities? What are the differences?	They both . . . They are different because . . .

ACADEMIC CONVERSATIONS IN SOCIAL STUDIES AND HISTORY

Social studies and history lessons can be opportunities for students to make connections to their lives as they discuss topics with others. Teachers can provide prompts that encourage students to bring their experiences, issues, and heritage into the classroom. They can also help students see that they can contribute to making the world a better place. Perspectives of people from different socioeconomic classes, genders, racial groups, ethnicities, and linguistic backgrounds can be shared. Students need to learn how history and social topics can be told from different points of view and that more inclusive stories of "less famous" people are also valuable.

You can emphasize three main types of conversations in social studies: (1) deciding between two sides of an issue, (2) collaborating to solve a problem, and (3) collaborating to explain causes, effects, and importance of events, people, traditions, and beliefs.

SS/History Type I: Deciding Between Two Sides of an Issue

Social studies and history offer a wide range of controversial issues that students can discuss. These topics can overlap with topics that emerge in language arts and science lessons, but here we highlight how sociologists and historians tend to talk about two-sided issues. As we covered in the first two chapters, students build up both sides of the issue with examples, evidence, and reasons. They will often need help from you in the form of read-alouds, visuals, and posters to both build their background knowledge and organize their ideas for and during conversations.

As children get older, their argumentation skills develop, especially their abilities to reason, to evaluate abstract evidence, and to explain how evidence supports a claim. In primary grades, teachers must help students have a solid foundation for arguing about social and historical topics. This foundation includes not deciding right away what side you are on but working together to build up one side and then the other, which they do by clarifying and supporting each side with evidence and examples.

Before their conversations, students need to have an idea of which two sides to talk about and some examples to support each side. You should model with another student how to build up both sides (you can use the Argument Balance Scale in Chapter 2). You can provide language frames such as "Let's build up one side first." "What is an example that supports that?"

Now take a look at this conversation in kindergarten about whether it is better to live in the city or the country. As a class, they had put some examples (words and pictures) onto a T-chart to help them in their conversations.

Brenda: Let's start with country.

Varun: Why is it good?

Brenda: No pollution. No cars, no car smoke. Good air.

Varun: Yeah. And food is fresh.

Brenda: What's an example?

Varun: Like milk. You get it right from a cow.

Brenda: And it's quiet. The city it's loud and lots of cars.

Varun: But cities are good, too.

Brenda: Why?

Varun: I don't know.

Brenda: Look up there (at the T-chart).

Varun: They, they got lots of stores.

Brenda: And jobs, and friends live close.

Varun: And there are movies and restaurants.

Brenda: So what's better?

Varun: I think city.

Varun: Me, too.

Notice how the T-chart helped them come up with ideas, and notice how they built up one idea first and then the second one. They had plenty of good back-and-forth turns, building on one another. Their turns could be longer, with more description, but this is still a strong conversation for kindergarten students. Imagine if these students keep having such conversations every day for years and years; a whole new type of student might leave our schools.

Here are a few other topics that can fit into social studies or history lessons.

- Do we learn from history or not?
- Is homework harmful or helpful to kids in our grade level?
- Are video games good or bad for you?
- What household chores should kids do or not do?
- Should animals be kept in cages (in zoos)?
- Are kids over-influenced by what other kids are wearing?
- Should cartoon card games be allowed in schools?
- Are school uniforms good or bad?
- Is the Internet good or bad for kids our age?
- Are athletes, actors, singers, or politicians good role models?
- Should junk food be banned from schools?

- Which is better, television or books?

- Should we stop exploring space?

- Should computers replace teachers?

SS/History Type 2: Collaborating to Solve Social Problems and Challenges

This type of conversation is more focused on collaborative critical thinking and creativity to practice solving (and some cases solving) social problems and challenges on different levels. In an activity we call Creativity Conversations, students pair up and engage in creative problem solving. Students learn to collaborate to engage in various stages of creativity, also referred to as *design thinking*. Problems are posed or chosen by students who then jointly discuss ideas based on the following steps:

1. Pick a topic that requires a creative way to solve a problem or express a complex idea to others. Give options, if possible (e.g., increasing how we show respect and responsibility at our school, dealing with bullies at school, reducing cheating in school, reducing the use of bad language, reducing the use of violent video games by students in school, solving a local pollution problem, helping homeless people, saving the rainforests).

2. Model for students the collaborative creativity process:

   - Clarify the problem. Students make sure they both can define the problem to others, describe why it is a problem, and explain what will change if the problem is solved.

   - Brainstorm possible solution ideas without critique. Any idea, within reason, is accepted and written down. This can be done as a whole class at first, and then eventually students will do this individually.

   - Narrow the solution ideas down with critical thinking and criteria. Have students decide if it is possible to use any of the solutions. They can talk about the high cost of certain solutions, and so on.

   - Zoom in on two solution ideas and then compare their merits, limits, rationales, evidence, potentials, and any past similar examples that worked or didn't.

   - Work together to choose the best solution and discuss how to implement it.

Have students collaborate to create or write their idea for a realistic audience.

Here is a first-grade example that focuses on the problem of pollution in the ocean. The teacher had read aloud a short article on the damage to wildlife caused by pollution. The problem-solving steps are up on the wall in words and images.

Naomi: So the problem is the plastic and garbage in the ocean.

Armando: It kills all fish and birds and—

Naomi: Not all of them; lots but not all.

Armando: That's what I mean.

Naomi: So how to solve it?

Armando: Tell people not to throw stuff out.

Naomi: You mean keep the garbage at home?

Armando: I mean not throw on the street. It goes in rivers to the ocean.

Naomi: Yeah, but tell them how? Like on TV?

Armando: Yeah.

Naomi: But the teacher said it costs money.

Armando: And maybe they don't listen.

Naomi: Maybe put nets on the rivers, like, to catch the garbage.

Armando: Hmmm. They cost money, but maybe less.

Naomi: They catch the bottles and stuff, and—

Armando: But what about boats? They might get stuck, *enredado* (tangled).

Naomi: Maybe they can lift it up the nets, like the bridges.

Armando: OK, we're done.

SS/History Type 3: Collaborating to Explain Events, Systems, and People

Yes, this type covers a lot of important ground, but so do history and social studies. This is the most common type of conversation found in social studies and history lessons. Historians tend to interpret events in the past and try to argue their causes and effects. Sociologists tend to study what groups of people do to live and grow together, which includes government and other social systems. And both (historians and sociologists) try to explain past and present people, including their importance, motivations, relationships, traditions, and beliefs. Exciting, right? And we have the privilege of helping students get an early start on developing their abilities to have these types of rich conversations.

A key element of this type of conversation is the prompt. When you have a good idea of what you want students to talk about, you can generate a helpful prompt. Here are a few examples:

- What point of view is this version of history showing?

- Whose story is not being told? How can we learn more about ordinary people? Should we learn about ordinary people?

- What helped George Washington to be chosen as the first president?

- Why did people back then get sick more often than now?

- What motivates people to move to different cities and countries?

- What is injustice and how can we make our country a better place?

- Why does Martin Luther King Jr. have a holiday?

- Why should we be respectful of others and their property?

- Why did Christopher Columbus sail across the Atlantic Ocean?

- Should we vote on every decision in our class?

- Why should we tell the truth?

- Is everything on the Internet true?

And here is a conversation in second grade that was prompted by "What does it mean to be a good citizen of this classroom, this country, and the world?"

Alexis: You gotta vote.

Daniel: Why?

Alexis: Cuz you just do.

Daniel: Yeah, but why?

Alexis: I think so that we don't, we get what we want. It's fair.

Daniel: Yeah.

Alexis: OK, what else. Like in our class?

Daniel: Be nice and don't steal.

Alexis: OK. And don't be a bully, and don't cheat.

Daniel: What about the country?

Alexis: Vote, like we said. Pay the taxes?

Daniel: Yeah, but I also think it means helping people, like poor people.

Alexis: How?

Daniel: I don't know. Maybe give them money or job or food.

Alexis: My auntie does that. She goes to some food place for homeless people. She gives them food.

Daniel: And world?

Alexis: We gotta help poor people. Clothes and doctors to help them.

Daniel: How?

Alexis: I don't know. Give money, or go see them?

Notice in this conversation the many clarification prompts that pushed students to share more about the various ideas. This shows how simple why and how questions can help sustain and deepen the conversation, allowing students to build and negotiate meanings. A suggestion for these students might be to use more examples to support their ideas.

Sample Academic Conversation Lesson Plan for Social Studies

This is a lesson plan that fosters skills for having SS/History Type 3 conversations. For this lesson within a unit on identity, students create an Identity Box. The boxes are filled with artifacts representing the students' background, family traditions, and heritage. Each student writes a paragraph to explain the contents of the box. Then students present their box initially to a partner. Finally, they present to the class and invited guests. By emphasizing oral language over written production, students are able to express more complex ideas and share deeper thoughts and understandings about their identities.

Grade: 2

Standards Addressed

- Massachusetts History and Social Science Curriculum Framework 2.8: With the help of a school librarian, give examples of traditions or customs from other countries that can be found in America today.

- CCSS.ELA-Literacy.CCRA.SL.1: Prepare for and participate effectively in a range of conversations and collaborations with diverse partners, building on others' ideas and expressing their own clearly and persuasively.

- CCSS.ELA-Literacy.CCRA.SL.2: Integrate and evaluate information presented in diverse media and formats, including visually, quantitatively, and orally.

- CCSS.ELA-Literacy.CCRA.SL.4: Present information, findings, and supporting evidence such that listeners can follow the line of reasoning and the organization, development, and style are appropriate to task, purpose, and audience.

Objectives

- Describe their various group identities.
- Analyze how identities are represented in *The Name Jar* (Yangsook Choi).
- Clarify your identity by talking with a partner.

Performance Assessment

- Present the identity box.

(Continued)

(Continued)

Lesson Sequence

Introduce skill, build background, and clarify an idea

- Introduce objectives.

- Teach the word "identity." Include the terms "gender," "race," "religion" and "language." Model how to talk about identities and what makes you who you are.

- Teach gesture and icon for CREATE. We will be creating and defining our own identity.

- Build background: Read aloud *The Name Jar*.

- Brainstorm words that identify the main character. Briefly highlight stereotypes and warn against judging people based on a single characteristic. For instance, being a girl doesn't necessarily mean you like to wear dresses; being a boy doesn't necessarily mean you like to play sports.

- Students can draw several artifacts that represent their identity. These are artifacts that they may be able to include in an identity box that can be shared with the class.

- Teacher models a conversation with a student about the artifacts.

- Academic conversation: Turn to your partner and ask, "What artifacts represent your identity?" You will be asked to share back your partner's ideas.

- Share back with the group. What did your partner explain about his or her identity? How are you similar? How are you different?

Review and Assessment

- Teacher gives formal evaluation of presentation of identity box.

Extension or Home-School Connection

- Students collect artifacts to put in their identity box. They discuss with family members how these items are symbols of identity.

Later in the school year, the second graders read biographies about famous people in history. Then they shared their learning during academic conversations and written reading responses. These students are WIDA levels 3 or 4 in speaking. The prompt is "What did you learn from your biography?" This is an excerpt from a longer conversation that lasted for over 12 minutes. Notice in this conversation how the second graders are able to go back to the text to find evidence for ideas.

Sandra: I learned that George Washington wants to be a soldier like Lawrence because he was in the . . . in the army. And he wants to be like the leader.

Tomas: When he was a kid, in this book, in the beginning, he was like . . . surprised . . . because he was visiting Lawrence. He and Lawrence were at the house.

Sandra: I know that, I heard that George is two feet, two and a half feet tall.

Tomas: Did you check in the book?

Sandra: Wait . . . *(Flips through book.)*

Tomas: *(Points at sentence.)*

Sandra: He was six feet, two inches tall.

Tomas: And when he was big, he was in the army, too. And he leaded the army to fight in the . . .

Sandra: He wanted to be a soldier like the "Lobsterbacks" cuz in the book that I read, the colonists had to fight with England and George Washington had to lead the military and had to be the leader of the colonists.

Tomas: And later on, he left the army and he went back to Mount Vernon, but not alone. Because then he met Martha.

Sandra: He met Martha Custis.

Tomas: Yeah. Custis. Then they went back to Mount Vernon.

By analyzing this conversation, we see that the students used academic vocabulary and sequence phrases including "when he was a kid," "in the beginning," "later on," and "then." They also used cause-and-effect terms; for example, "He wanted to be a soldier like the 'Lobsterbacks' cuz in the book that I read, the colonists had to fight with England." With more instruction in the language of cause and effect, these students can further their thinking and reasoning. It's important to note that these two students developed conversational stamina over the course of the year.

ACTIVITIES FOR BUILDING THE SKILL OF CONVERSATIONS IN SOCIAL STUDIES

- **Think-Puzzle-Explore** (adapted from Ritchhart, Church, & Morrison, 2011). Students ask their partners and then report back to the group: "What do you think you know about this topic? What questions or puzzles do you have? How can we explore the puzzles we have about this topic?" This is a starting point for inquiry projects. By explaining what they think they know, students can gain confidence in the topic and build background knowledge.

- **Tackle History's Big Questions.** Look for mysteries, controversies, and big questions within the topic. Have students generate their own big questions and converse about how to research the answers. For example, "How did Pocahontas feel?" "Why did settlers travel West?" "Did George Washington follow the core values of our school?"

- **Opinion Continuum.** (See description in Chapter 2.) Ask students a question that they can take a stance on. For example, "Is July 4th an important holiday?"

Core Skills and Terms in Social Studies & History	Sample Questions	Sample Responses
Cause and effect one reason, therefore, as a result	What were some causes of the conflict? Why did people immigrate?	The causes were . . . Some reasons were . . .
Recognize perspective point of view, evidence, examples	Who is the author? Where did this artifact come from?	It was written because . . . This illustrates . . .
Compare alike, different, similar, both, in comparison	How are these leaders similar? Is this tradition different from other traditions?	They both . . . They are different because . . .
Evaluate therefore, in conclusion, finally, evidence shows	Which was most important? What is the main result?	The most important . . . As a result . . .

ACADEMIC CONVERSATIONS IN MATH

Learning is different across the content areas, but learning in math can be even more different. Learning new math concepts tends to depend heavily on the learning of previous concepts. For example, if a child doesn't know one-to-one correspondence (i.e., only count one thing once when counting a set of things), she will have trouble adding two numbers. Math learning usually involves solving a wide variety of problems in various forms that use numbers, symbols, pictures, and/or words.

We also must try to undo some of the common myths surrounding math learning: (1) you need to solve problems quickly, (2) mistakes are bad, and (3) you need to work individually. Fortunately, conversation work can help with all three. They allow students to take more time to solve and think about problems, to share and learn from their mistakes and those of others, and they work with peers. And yet, conversation work in math is no walk in the park; it doesn't just happen. It takes effort to foster productive conversations and go beyond the common "the stronger math student in the pair solves it and lets the partner copy" strategy.

One major shift we are trying to foster is going from an emphasis on just getting the right answer (whether or not you understand the math behind it) to an emphasis on understanding, using multiple methods, and communicating your thinking to others. The right answer is just a part of what we are asking students to do. Conversations are a powerful way to engage in this shift.

New standards emphasize communicating mathematical thinking to others. For example, CCSS Mathematical Practice Standard 3 states: Construct viable arguments and critique the reasoning of others. As students listen and respond to their peers, they can clarify their own thinking and help others. And teachers also can learn about misunderstandings during their conversations.

There are many types of conversations in math. Here we highlight just three: (1) collaborating to solve a problem, (2) collaborating to create new math problems, and (3) experimenting with math ideas, numbers, and shapes.

Math Type I: Collaborating to Solve a Problem

Yes, this type of math conversation is the most common—and may even be overused. It is important, however, for students to learn how to talk with each other to solve problems. The sharing and critiquing and justifying of ideas during conversations can accelerate students' mathematical language development. And often students are more engaged in math when working with (not copying from) others.

Students can learn to use the *Math Paired Conversation Protocol*, outlined here, to scaffold their conversations. Here are the steps

1. Collaboratively clarify the problem. Make sure students know what the terms mean in the problem, what is happening, and what the problem asks for.

2. Each student estimates the answer and justifies the estimate.

3. Then they brainstorm ways to begin solving the problem. They don't criticize the ideas. They have to come up with at least two possible methods.

4. They choose a method; one student moves the objects or writes down the process while the other keeps asking why—even if he or she knows why. This allows for verbalization of ideas and justifications.

5. Then the other student writes for Step 4 with the other method.

6. They then compare their answers and their methods and fix any problems.

7. They can practice the statement "With problems like these, you can solve them in two ways. One way is . . . and the other is . . . Notice how they are similar in that . . ."

8. They also compare their answers to their estimates.

Here is a first-grade conversation about algebraic thinking. The teacher read aloud and acted out the problem: "Seven frogs lived in a pond. Yesterday more frogs arrived from a nearby lake. Now there are 12 frogs total! How many new frogs arrived yesterday?" The teacher asked them to talk with partners about how to solve it.

Israel: I say just plus them.

May: Why?

Israel: Cause those are the numbers.

May: But it says now 12 frogs. Seven more is too many.

Israel: So minus 'em?

May: Why? They didn't leave.

Israel: Cuz they are the numbers.

May: We can draw it. Here's the pond. Seven frogs in it. Then plus what?

Israel: We don't know. But now 12. Maybe count.

May: I can draw them and count them.

Israel: Here's seven. Now 8, 9, 10, 11, 12.

May: So 1, 2, 3, 4, 5. It's 5 new frogs.

Notice that May, at least, used the skill of prompting for support of ideas when she asked "Why?" twice. This helped them both think about what was happening in the problem and think about why they would use the operations that they had learned. They could have tried both addition and subtraction and then guessed which answer made more sense, but they wouldn't have understood the math they were supposed to use based on the problem. By talking about it and breaking it down into the drawing, they had a much better start at the algebraic thinking they were supposed to develop.

Critique, Clarify, and Correct. Another variation of this type of conversation is a conversation about a flawed response. It is a way for students to talk about where a fictitious student (David) went wrong in the solving of a problem. You observe students for common errors in reasoning that they make when solving problems. Then you create a student name and write down the "student's" work for a problem, including the flawed reasoning. Then your real students pair up and you ask them to work together to come up with some recommendations for David to help him understand the math he needs to do the problem. They clarify the problem and what David did wrong, then they clarify how to do the problem in one or more correct ways. Here is an example from third grade.

Sara: He added them, the two numbers.

Carlos: Why?

Sara: I don't know. Maybe he thought it was easier.

Carlos: But the problem it says "she bought 6 packages and each package had 5 cookies in it."

Sara: He got eleven, but there's more, right?

Carlos: He should draw it. Like to see it more, that's more of them. Like this (draws 6 squares with 5 circles in each). Then count them up. 1, 2 . . . 30.

Sara: But multiply works, too. 6 times 5. That's 30.

Carlos: So what do we tell him?

Sara: He can draw it, like that, or multiply. I think multiply cuz it's faster.

Carlos: But you gotta know them, too. Like know 5 times 6 is 30.

Notice how this type of conversation helps students be teachers, in a sense, and take a slightly different perspective on the math and reasoning needed for problem solving. When they are focused on helping someone else understand the math, they are less myopically focused on solving their own problem as quickly as possible (which is an all-too-common mindset in math in school). They work together to come up with a clear way to make suggestions to the fictitious student and learn about common flaws along the way.

Math Type 2: Collaborating to Create New Math Problems

This type of math conversation is much rarer than the other two because students are not often allowed to be creative and come up with their own problems in math curricula and lessons. However, the benefits are worth the time. Why? Many students desire to add their creativity and interests to learning, which means they put more energy (and learning) into the process. When they work with another student to create a problem, they need to negotiate both language and math at the same time. That is, they both work on language to clarify what is happening in the problem, making it clear enough for others in the class to understand and solve.

To create problems, students must apply the math they have learned to real-world settings, in a sense, reverse engineering the problems and thereby building a better understanding of how different kinds of problems work. For example, if we tell you right now to create a problem that requires using multiplication of fractions, you immediately need to think of and describe a setting that uses fractions. Then you need to think about what would happen in the problem to require multiplying rather than addition, subtraction, division, and so on. Here is an example from second grade:

Leo: We gotta do a story problem with addition and subtraction.

Ali: OK. We can do a store.

Leo: How?

Ali: We go to store for food. We buy two things like—

Leo: Like cookies and ice cream, lots. I'm hungry.

Ali: OK, then what?

Leo: The numbers, prices. So maybe cookies cost 15 dollars and ice cream 18 dollars.

Ali: I like to break cookies on ice cream.

Leo: Yeah, but the problem. The teacher is coming.

Ali: We gotta write the problem first. So what we ask?

Leo: How 'bout "The teacher went to the store to buy cookies and ice cream for her students. The cookies cost 15 dollars and the ice cream 18. How much is it?"

Ali: What about minus, subtract?

Leo: Oh yeah. Maybe she eats 10.

Ali: 10 what? Dollars? No. Maybe she pay too much and get change . . . like my mom.

Leo: She pays $50, OK? That's more than it.

Ali: So we put, "She pays $50. How much change she get back?"

Leo: Write "did she get back?"

Notice how this type of conversation also helps students be teachers. When they are creating their own math problem, they need to use language as a tool to create. They collaborate and use their background knowledge of numbers (in this case money) to design a question. As they converse, they refine their language at the word, sentence, and message levels. They also enjoy the companionship of working with a peer and add humor to their math problem. Who doesn't like discussing cookies and ice cream?

Math Type 3: Modeling Math Concepts and Experimenting with Numbers, Symbols, and Shapes

This type of conversation has more variation than the others. It is not focused on solving or creating problems, but rather on showing and experimenting with math ideas. It is also rare that teachers give students time to "play with" math ideas. These conversations are focused on clarifying and exploring understandings, which can be foundational for many students. For example, you might have two students work together to come up with a presentation for other students on the topic of regrouping during subtraction. Students play with different examples and try to show, with objects and/or drawings, the idea of regrouping, why it's done, and how. Here is a sample conversation from second grade based on this task.

Eli:	Like the teacher said, start with Why? Why regroup?
Thomas:	Cuz you don't have enough. Like say it's 25 over 28. You can't take five from eight. You gotta regroup.
Eli:	But 28's too big to take from 25.
Thomas:	Oh yeah. Then 35, not 25. That works
Eli:	So what do we show?
Thomas:	That the 3 is actually not just 3.
Eli:	It's 30.
Thomas:	So you regroup. Get 10 from it and you got 20 left, but just put 2 there. I put 20 there one time and messed up.
Eli:	Ok, the 10, then what?
Thomas:	Add it here (to the 5), so you got 15 on top to minus the 8. It's big enough now.
Eli:	But did we change the number? I don't think we can change it?
Thomas:	Add it to see.
Eli:	2 plus—
Thomas:	It's 20.
Eli:	20 plus the 15, it's . . . 35, so it's the same.
Thomas:	Then minus the 2 minus 2 and you, it's 0. So 7 is the answer.
Eli:	Now the poster to make.

Notice how these students delved into the conceptual reasoning needed to understand regrouping as they prepared to explain it to others. They made up their own problem as a model and used plenty of language along the way. They even checked their thinking when Thomas said to add up the new parts they had made from 35, grounding this idea in a key mathematical principle that you can't change the value of numbers (which will serve them well later on, too). Think about how the conversation likely helped prepare them with the poster they were about to cocreate.

Take a moment to think about how your students might work together to model the math they are currently learning, or to experiment and "play" with math concepts and tools to understand them without the pressure of solving a problem. Other tasks could include:

- Design a poster that explains multiplication.

- Show how to "take apart" numbers using addition and subtraction.

- Show different ways to count or group objects, but always counting an object once.

- See how many shapes and what types of shapes you can make by cutting up larger shapes.

- Measure things in the room and see which things have the same measurements.

- Brainstorm 10 ways to use math in the real world.

- Plan a party for the class and estimate what it will cost.

Sample Academic Conversation Lesson Plan for Math

In the following lesson plan, students are asked to model the "taking apart" of a number to understand that other numbers can be added together to make a number. The language function is to explain mathematical thinking by sequencing steps. A secondary language objective could be to ask questions to prompt further explanation of problem solving. Students need to be able to ask, "How did you take them apart?" (inserting the direct pronoun in the phrase) and "What did you do next?" How would you include language in the objective?

Grade: Kindergarten
Standards Addressed K.OA.I: Represent addition and subtraction with objects, fingers, mental images, drawings, sounds.
Objectives Represent decomposition addition stories to six with blocks with no unknown.
Performance Assessment Paired conversations about the concept of taking apart a number.
Lesson Sequence *Introduce skill, build background, and create an idea* • Introduce language and content objectives. • Build background—Remind students about how we "put together" numbers previously. • Teach phrase and gesture for "take apart" and say, "Today we will take apart the number six." • Draw on board: *If six teddy bears are sitting on the bed and three fall off, how many are left sitting on the bed?* • Students write on their white boards and also practice with linking cubes. • What did we get? A student comes up and shows how to get three. "Notice how we can take six apart and get three and three." • Then say that there are other numbers we can get when we take six apart. For example, "If two teddy bears fall off the bed, how many are left?" Let's have conversations.

- Fishbowl modeling: Teacher and a student introduce prompts: "What did you take apart? Why did you take it apart? How did you take it apart?" and "Are there any other ways to take it apart?"

Student: What did you take apart and how you did it?

Teacher: For the first problem I took apart six and got three and three.

Student: Why?

Teacher: Because in the problem it says that three fell off the bed. What about you?

Student: How did you do it?

Teacher: I counted three blocks and moved them from the bed to the floor like this: one, two, three. And counted the ones that were left, one, two, three. So what did you take apart when two fell off the bed?

Student: Six.

Teacher: Why did you do that?

Student: Cuz six bears started on the bed.

Teacher: How did you get your answer?

Student: I erased two bears from my board. See? And got four left.

Teacher: I like your thinking. Are there any other ways to take six apart?

Student: I don't know.

Teacher: What if five bears fall from the bed?

- Teacher asks class: "What did you notice from this conversation?" (Asked each other what, why, and how questions to understand math thinking and reasons for doing things. Each person had different strategies for solving.)
- Prompts and sentence starters for "take apart" are displayed up front. Students also have boards with dry erase markers to show their work.
- Students engage in paired conversations similar to the fishbowl model. (Teacher introduces a new problem starting with six balls on a shelf.)
- Teacher observes and provides feedback to pairs.

Review and Assessment

Teacher informally analyzes use of term "take apart" and completed number groups that make up the number 6.

Here is a sample conversation focused on taking apart numbers. In this lesson, two kindergarten students converse about taking apart numbers to understand subtraction and addition. The teacher gave different cards to each student in a pair, one in which one apple fell and one in which four apples fell. She put what, why, and how question starters up on the wall to scaffold their conversations.

Dana: What did you take apart?

Tran: Six.

Dana: Why you take it apart?

Tran: Six apples on tree. Here.

Dana: What did you do?

Tran: I take apart six.

Dana: How?

Tran: One fall so I move it down here. Five stay.

Dana: Good. Now ask me.

Tran: What you take apart?

Dana: Six.

Tran: Why?

Dana: There's six apples on it.

Tran: What did you do?

Dana: I took apart six.

Tran: Why?

Dana: Because there's six on the tree. Then four falled off. Just two now.

Tran: How?

Dana: Look. These four, I drawed [arrows] down, and I erase 'em. Then counted two up here now.

Notice how the two structures for the conversation helped. First there was an information gap in that they had different problems to share. Second, the what, why, and how questions helped extend the conversation to provide practice in using math language to share thinking. In this conversation, students were able to use the target vocabulary with some accuracy, but still could improve in their use of sentences.

The teacher has the important job of listening carefully to the language that the students produce during the academic conversations in math (we dive into assessment in the next chapter). The teacher should listen to their mathematical reasoning as well as their uses of vocabulary, grammar, and communication skills. Humphries and Parker (2015) write, "This is the challenge—and joy—of *teaching by listening* to students" (p. 17). Teachers learn as they teach.

ACTIVITIES FOR BUILDING THE SKILL OF ACADEMIC CONVERSATIONS IN MATH

- **"Stronger & Clearer Each Time Grid."** Give students a challenging word problem to solve. Give them time to read it (or read it aloud to them) and think about how they might solve it. Some might solve it right away and others not. Their ultimate goal is to be able to clearly explain their method(s) for solving it. They circulate to ask three different classmates, "Which strategy did you use to solve this problem? Why?" Record the answers on the interview grid.

Name	Strategy and Answer

- **See-Think-Wonder** (adapted from Ritchhart, Church, & Morrison, 2011). Draw a mathematical array or illustrate a math problem on the board. Students ask a partner, "What do you see?" Report back to whole class. Then, "What do you think?" Report back to whole class. Finally, "What do you wonder?" Report back to whole class.

- **What & Why Information Gap Math Cards.** In this activity, Partner A has the general problem or situation on one card and Partner B has the information needed to solve it on the "data card." Data cards can also contain diagrams, tables, graphs, and other information. Partner A needs to realize what is needed and ask for information that is provided on Partner B's data card. (The data card can contain unnecessary information.) There is an information gap, and students need to orally exchange information to bridge the gap. Partner B should not share information (a) unless

(Continued)

(Continued)

Partner A specifically asks for it, and (b) after A says why the information is needed. Neither partner should read their cards to one another or show their cards to their partners. As they work the problem, they justify their responses using clear and connected language. Procedure:

1. The problem card partner (Partner A) reads his or her card silently and thinks aloud about what information is needed. Partner B reads the data card silently.

2. Partner B asks, "What specific information do you need?" Partner A needs to ask for specific information from Partner B.

3. When Partner A asks, Partner B should ask for justification—"Why do you need that information?"—before telling it to Partner A.

4. Partner A then explains how he or she is using the information to solve the problem. Partner B helps and asks for explanations, even if he or she understands what Partner A is doing.

5. As a follow-up step, have both students use blank cards to write their own similar problem card and data card for other pairs to use.

Emma wants to buy two new shirts at the store. She had some money that she made by selling lemonade on the corner last Sunday. Does she have enough money?	The red shirt costs 9 dollars. The green shirt costs 12 dollars. The pants cost 16 dollars. The store is 3 miles away. Emma made 20 dollars last Sunday.

Figure 4.1   Sample Info-Gap Math Cards

ACADEMIC CONVERSATIONS IN ART

Specialist teachers, including art, music, physical education, and health, have important roles to play in promoting student interaction. Through academic conversations, all teachers can encourage students to learn from each other as they explore new ideas. Our art teacher colleagues explained that there are several main types of conversations in art: (1) determining the meaning of the artwork or the intent of the artist, (2) comparing personal responses and emotional reactions to art, and (3) analyzing the artistic process and materials using elements of art and principles of design. Conversations among young artists reveal their interpretations of beauty and creative work across different media.

Sample Academic Conversation Lesson Plan for Art

This lesson plan provides an opportunity for an Art Type 2 discussion. Students can compare their personal responses to art. The focus on disagreeing may be too negative for some classrooms, and you may want to shift to a focus on "I understand your perspective and I'd like to add my own." Or "I hear what you are saying, but I see . . ." The language function is to state an opinion and to support ideas with evidence. The teacher in this lesson made clear and detailed language objectives to align with the language function. Not all these need to be posted and reviewed for the students, but they provide the teacher with a road map for the lesson and what the expectations are.

Grade: 2
Unit: Analyzing themes in artwork

Standards Addressed

MA Visual Arts: 5.1. In the course of making and viewing art, learn ways of discussing it, such as by making a list of all of the images seen in an artwork (visual inventory) and identifying kinds of color, line, texture, shapes, and forms in the work.

Objectives

- Describe artwork using descriptive details.
- Name the skill—EVALUATE-COMPARE-CHOOSE.
- Define the skill and explain when it is used.
- Use the Visual Thinking Strategy sentence starter to describe a painting: "I think that _____ because I see _____."
- Build on a partner's idea by using the sentence starter "I would add that . . ." or "I agree with you because . . ."
- Challenge a partner's idea by using the sentence starter "I see it a different way . . ." or "From my point of view . . ."

Performance Assessment

Paired conversations about the meaning of a work of visual art.

Lesson Sequence

Introduce skill, build background, and create an idea

- "Today we will practice the academic conversation skill of EVALUATE-COMPARE-CHOOSE. It is also important to add to others' ideas to show you are listening to them."

- Teach icon and hand gesture. Evidence supports and contributes to a strong foundation.

- Review the norms for conversations:

  a. I question ideas, not people.

  b. I listen respectfully to all ideas, even if I disagree.

  c. I know other students may disagree with me, but I'm still an important person.

  d. I might change my mind during the conversation.

- Teach: What makes you think that? In the artwork there is . . . and this supports the idea because . . .

- Show a piece of artwork that has a theme.

- Whole class discussion about the painting using sentence starters for describing the painting, "I think that _____ because I see _____" and for agreeing.

- Teach how to challenge or respectfully disagree. "I see it a different way . . ." or "I respectfully disagree because . . ."

- Whole class discussion about the painting, practicing disagreeing in a respectful way, using the sentence starters.

- Partner practice. Have a conversation about a new piece of artwork. Come up with one or two themes and the evidence for them.

- Review with class.

Review and Assessment

Exit ticket. Did you feel that your ideas were valuable, even if your partner did not agree with you?

Extension or Home-School Connection

Students have an academic conversation at home with a family member about a piece of art: What do you see in this artwork?

Report back to class on answers.

Here is a sample conversation from the lesson. The teacher first had students describe what is happening and then move on to the meanings.

Max: It shows a bunch of kids playing. They're on a farm.

Lia: Yeah, with rocks or something.

Max: Maybe marbles. And little kids watching them.

Lia: They're having fun, laughing. And a boy is painting.

Max: What's the meaning?

Lia: To show kids having fun?

Max: Yeah. I don't know. And they don't have video games.

Lia: Maybe that's it. It shows that kids can have fun without video games or TV.

Max: And maybe that kids do art, too, like the boy.

Lia: You mean, kids *should* do art, maybe instead of TV?

Max: Yeah.

Lia: So it means we should do art and—

Max: And kids can have fun without video games and TV.

Notice the students' use of interpretation as they talked about the meaning of the painting. Whether or not it was the artist's intention, these students, through conversation, were able to practice their interpretation of themes, which will help them in the future for visual and written texts. They also do some clarifying of language when Lia says, "You mean, kids *should* do art, maybe instead of TV?"

CHAPTER SUMMARY

Many districts are emphasizing schoolwide goals that focus on increasing engagement, articulating thinking, and fostering empathy and compassion. By incorporating daily academic conversations across disciplines, teachers can ensure that students are developing the communication skills they need to be successful in school and in life. Different disciplines have different types of conversations, and it helps to know the main ones, what they look and sound like, and how to best foster them.

PLC PROMPTS FOCUSED ON
CONVERSATIONS IN THE CONTENT AREAS

- What are the main types of conversations in your content area? Which type are students skilled at? Which type do they need more practice or support in?

- How can conversations in a discipline help students learn key concepts and skills of that discipline?

- Choose a type of conversation to implement in your content area. Share samples of student conversations to analyze with your colleagues.

ASSESSING STUDENT CONVERSATIONS

If you don't know where you are, you'll have a hard time getting to your destination.

While educational policy has increased standardized testing mandates in recent years, teachers can capture the power of assessing and providing feedback through formative assessments. Gottlieb and Willner (2016) distinguish between assessment *for* learning, assessment *as* learning, and assessment *of* learning.

Assessment *for* learning is formative assessment. Formative assessment means using observation and analysis skills to see how well students have learned what they are supposed to learn and what more they need to do and learn. Formative assessment is a skill, not a stack of short quizzes or essays. In fact, all assessments should be formative. The evidence gained in formative assessment is used to inform instruction.

Assessment *as* learning happens as students reflect on their own learning and self-assess how they are approaching, meeting, or exceeding the objectives for the lesson or unit. The assessment task or process actually helps students further learn content or develop skills. In this case, conversations that are assessed tend to help learning, even though they are being assessed.

Summative assessments, including things like standardized tests, tend to be in the category of assessment *of* learning. Even though these assessments are typically long, end-of-year, multiple-choice tests, some teachers we know have begun to have summative-like assessments of conversation. These are end-of-semester and end-of-year assessments in which the teacher more or less randomly pairs students to have a conversation about a recent topic of study or essential question.

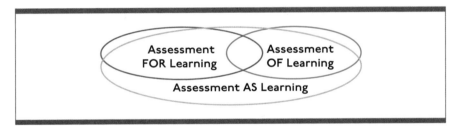

Three main spheres of assessment.

As you can see by this diagram, most conversations are not just one type. We even argue that conversations are unique in that almost all of them can be educational, which is why the assessment *as* learning oval is so large. Even if a conversation is being assessed, it tends to provide the student with new information and practice in conversation skills. For example, a teacher observes two students talking about a social studies topic and notices that students need to clarify ideas more. The students, after using a self-assessment rubric, realize that they need to use better listening to respond to one another's turns. And both students realize that they learned new content from the other. We describe ways to engage in all three overlapping forms of assessment in this chapter.

WHY ANALYZE CONVERSATIONS?

We could spend several pages answering this question, but instead we just refer you to the description of the Conversation Observation and Analysis Tool in the next section. It explains the many things that conversations can show us about student learning.

ASSESSMENT *FOR* LEARNING: THE CONVERSATION OBSERVATION AND ANALYSIS TOOL (COAT)

Assessment *for* learning is a process used by teachers and students as part of instruction that provides feedback. During academic conversations, teachers listen carefully to students' use of language and content understandings. With this information, teachers adjust ongoing instruction to improve students' achievement of core content and language objectives.

On many occasions, we have seen teachers anxious to jump into conversations and "rescue" students by cueing them with ideas or vocabulary. However, this tool will help remind you that students have control over the conversations. The COAT provides you with information about where to take the next lesson and what scaffolding students may need. COAT can be used as a summative assessment (assessment *of* learning), but it was developed to be a formative tool. This observation tool covers a lot of conversation ground. The COAT, or whatever variation of it you prefer, can be on paper, but it should eventually be mostly in your head. There is too much to read through and check off as you are listening to two students in real time in a classroom setting. We recommend that you use it on paper for a while, even with recorded conversations that you can stop and re-listen to and then gradually try to observe conversations without it. Here is an annotated version with helpful questions to get you started.

Quantity

☐ # of turns

☐ Length of turns

☐ Equity of voice

- *Are there enough turns for a meaningful conversation?*
- *Is each turn long enough? Should they be longer with more sentences?*
- *Do both students talk more or less an equal amount? Does one student dominate?*

Quality

☐ Use conversation skills to co-construct and argue ideas

___ Turns build on previous turns

___ Students pose or choose a relevant initial idea(s) that is focused on learning objective(s)

___ Students clarify idea(s) (by paraphrasing, defining, elaborating, asking questions, negotiating, etc.)

___ Students support ideas (using evidence, examples, explanations)

- *Do students listen well enough to appropriately build on previous turns?*
- *Do students use posing, clarifying, and supporting ideas to build up one or more ideas?*

(Continued)

(Continued)

- *Do students build up both (or more) ideas as much as possible?*
- *Do students then evaluate the overall evidence weight of each side to make a logical decision?*
- *Do they clearly describe why they chose a side?*

- *Do students show effective listening by how they respond in each turn and nonverbally?*
- *Do students work hard to say things as clearly as possible each turn?*
- *Do they clearly describe why they chose a side?*
- *Do they use thinking skills needed to have a successful conversation?*
- *Do they use effective nonverbal skills for listening, emphasizing, questioning, and so on?*
- *Do they value (and not disrespect) one another's ideas?*

___ *If there are two or more competing ideas (argue/decide):*

students build up both ideas and

___ (a) evaluate the strength/weight of the evidence of each idea

___ (b) compare the strengths/weights and choose the "strongest/heaviest" idea

___ (c) explain and/or negotiate final decisions and conclusions

☐ Effective listening

☐ Clear speaking (plus use of language asked for in prompt)

☐ Academic thinking (including use of thinking asked for in prompt)

☐ Academic content (including talk about content asked for in prompt)

☐ Nonverbal communication (posture, nods, eye contact)

☐ Value one another's ideas, thinking, and feelings

 resources.corwin.com/ZwiersK3Guide

WAIT, THERE'S MORE!

The COAT contains the core set of elements that we tend to look for in academic conversations. However, here are several additional important dimensions of learning and development that conversations can help us see (adapted from Singer & Zwiers, 2016).

- **Perspectives.** Students often have a wide range of perspectives on topics, and conversations are great ways to understand them.

- **Connections:** Conversations offer insights into the types of connections and applications that students make to other contexts, content areas, texts, and life experiences.

- **Learning approaches and engagement:** How does the student approach learning in this discipline and learning in general? How engaged in the topic is he? What questions does he ask?

- **Power dynamics:** Which voices dominate discussions? Which students are silent, or defer to others to converse? Is participation equitable, or are there patterns by race, gender, English language learner, or other status that may factor into whose voice is heard?

As you can see, conversations can be very rich sources of information about students. You can get many important insights for the "price" of one analyzed conversation—and for at least two students at the same time!

"TRY ON THE COAT"

Here is a conversation from a second-grade classroom about the Day of the Dead. The teacher had read aloud a book about the holiday. The prompt, given by the teacher, was "Talk to your partner about the Day of the Dead and decide together what the message of the story was." Read through the conversation with the descriptions of quantity and quality in the COAT in mind. Try to come up with some strengths and an area or two that the students might need to work on.

1 Student A: Not to be sad; to be happy because it's a good thing to be in heaven, 'cause you get a lot of rest . . . like a lot of rest.

2 Student B: On the Day of the Dead you can celebrate your loved ones, and the song is also about you don't cry.

3 Student A: Also their loved ones are really . . . they're happy because they die, because they get lots of rest and they . . . mostly their ancestors and their families and friends and pets watch over them and make sure they're doing well.

4 Student B: And—

5 Student A: Right now, my Grandma Tutu is watching me.

6 Student B: And the kids were really wanting the special treats. The um . . . the sugar skull.

7 Student A: Also about the story there was . . . there was flowers and you could see the spirits in the pictures, in the designs in the book.

8 Student B: And when you're in heaven the angels watch after you.

9 Student A: Also you . . . in heaven sometimes you can . . . um when you're in heaven up there, you can watch over them, and you can see them, see them walking and praying; and you can also pray to heaven that you wish their family members or their family or their pets or their friends.

OK, what did you see with respect to quantity and quality on the COAT? We thought nine turns were solid, and the average length of turns was longer than typical for second grade. Student A shared a little more and even interrupted B in Line 5. Perhaps this is something to bring up to them or the whole class. Regarding the quality and building up their idea, we thought it was also solid; they referred to language and examples in the text and also a song that they had listened to. Student A even used a personal example in Line 5. They used plenty of rich language and focused on the content of the prompt; they used academic thinking in their interpretation and talk about abstract ideas such as watching after you, pray, heaven, and ancestors. And for the most part they valued one another's ideas—at least there was not obvious non-valuing or disrespecting of ideas. One thing to work on could be sticking to the main purpose and building it up. They could have tried to keep building up the idea that it's good to be in heaven and get lots of rest. There are many good ideas but they don't try to use them to support the initial idea, nor do they connect them in the end to answer the prompt.

YOU ARE AN ACTION RESEARCHER

Whether intentional or not, teachers do action research. Action research means that you focus on a problem or question and try to experiment with different interventions to see if and how much they make a difference. The action part means that you can take immediate action in your setting (e.g., classroom), based on your analysis of evidence and reflections, to improve learning in your setting. Action research is useful for the more challenging and messy questions that we have about learning, such as "How can we improve conversations in our classroom?"

As you already know all too well, you can't assess every conversation that happens in your lessons. In fact, this is the one of the biggest challenges that many teachers bring up in our work with them. It requires a hefty amount of strategic creativity to effectively assess conversations. Several strategies include:

- Creating a schedule of observations over 2 weeks so that you can observe full conversations for every student in the class.

- Creating a priority list that helps you observe students you are more concerned about, and you can even prioritize what you are looking for: language, conversation skills, content understandings, thinking skills, and so on.

- Experimenting with recording systems (phones, tablets, computers) and strategically sampling student conversations.

A second challenge is knowing what to do with the information you get from conversations. For example, you might have listened to a week's worth of conversations in your first-grade classroom. Student conversations seemed to be all over the place with a variety of strengths and needs. You need to train your ears and eyes to look for "patterns in the data" and "themes" that emerge. Often you will notice conversations skills that are strong or weak, content misunderstandings, lack of use of thinking skills, and so on. This skill takes a lot of time and practice—and a lot of student conversations. But with the knowledge gained in this book (and other similar resources), coupled with a few years of observation practice, your expertise in this area will develop to serve your students over time.

In the following three conversations, the pairs responded to the same prompt at the same time. Imagine you are the teacher and analyze these for patterns, using the COAT to guide your analyses. Students had read *Fish Is Fish* (Leoni) and were asked to talk about what they thought the author was trying to teach readers through the story.

#1

1 Student A: I think be who you are s'posed to be.

2 Student B: I think the lesson is uh . . . don't try to be same as others. Different is OK.

3 Student A: Why?

4 Student B: Because the fish tried to go up on the land, but he can't breathe. He's a fish.

5 Student A: I think that you have to be yourself.

6 Student B: Why?

7 Student A: Cuz my mom said it when we read a book.

8 Student B: Don't try to be like everyone else, too.

9 Student A: Yeah, what if they laugh at you?

#2

1 Student C: I think it's, um, good to be different than other animals; you shouldn't be like them. Because fish isn't a frog and—

2 Student D: I think we should try different things.

3 Student C: What do you mean?

4 Student D: Like fly and walk and see new places.

5 Student C: But he almost died.

6 Student D: Yeah, but—

7 Student C: I still think the author wants to teach us to be happy with us like we are.

8 Student D: OK.

#3

1 Student E: I think it's how to be friends.

2 Student F: That's a good idea. My idea is, I don't know how to say it. Like the fish saw the bird and cow like a fish. He never saw land things like them.

3 Student E: So what do we learn?

4 Student F: Maybe you gotta get out and see things like birds and cows.

5 Student E: I know what they look like.

6 Student F: Yeah. Me, too. But it's like going to space and seeing aliens.

7 Student E: How?

6 Student F: We think they got two legs and two arms and walk and are green. Maybe they're way different.

7 Student E: Yeah.

What patterns did you notice? There was a variety of ideas posed by students about the same text, and there was some solid turn-taking in each conversation.

There was also some effective clarifying and support of ideas in all three. One pattern of concern we noticed was that in all three conversations, the second student to talk posed his or her own idea rather than building up the first idea posed. They could have asked or helped clarify or support this first idea, but they posed their own idea instead. This effectively shifted the focus and built on to a second idea, leaving the first behind, and possibly, frustrating the students who posed them.

PROTOCOL FOR ANALYZING ACADEMIC CONVERSATIONS

This might help you better analyze student conversations, whether you are analyzing alone or with a group of teachers. After each section title, there are guiding questions, notes, and even some sentence starters to help spark reflective thinking and discussion. We encourage you to try this protocol as a way to use student work to improve conversation-based instruction. It is an alternative to analysis procedures that examine just one student artifact at a time. Teams look for patterns and trends across the group of students. Professional learning community (PLC) members suggest instructional strategies to address areas of need. Then the group reconvenes to notice if the new instruction has impacted student learning. This entire process is completed in cycles, always with the overarching inquiry question in mind.

I. **Pose an Inquiry Question:** This question format can be "How can I improve (some aspect of student conversations), evidenced by (one or more types of evidence), by (using a certain strategy or approach)?

II. **Clarify Expectations**: What learning do I want/expect students' conversations to show? Starters: I assume . . . I expect to see . . . I wonder . . . Some possibilities for learning that this data may present . . .

III. **Observe Patterns & Trends**: What are the general trends observed? Starters: Just the facts—"I observe that . . . Some patterns/trends that I notice . . . I counted . . . The percentage of . . . I'm surprised that I see . . ." (Avoid inferential terms such as "Because . . . Therefore . . . It seems . . . However . . .")

IV. **Make Interpretations:** What can we interpret and infer about student learning from the data? Starters: "I believe the data suggests _____ because . . . Perhaps _____ is causing the pattern of . . . I think the students need . . ."

V. **Ask Questions about the Data:** Usually, questions arise related to interpretations, such as "Why did these students do this? What can I still do to improve in this area? Is this data consistent and significant enough to change how I teach?"

(Continued)

(Continued)

VI. **Plan Solutions:** What are the implications for instruction and assessment? Starters: "We could try . . . because . . . This strategy or assessment would be most effective for this group . . . because . . ."

VII. **Plan What to Do and Bring for the Next Meeting:** If this is a PLC that works together on the inquiry question (which we highly recommend), then as a group you can decide what artifacts, evidence, and information would be most helpful for the next meeting. This also helps clarify what to do in the classroom to come up with such evidence or information. Two big questions: What are we going to teach? and how? (Possible formats: We could teach the same way and assess the same way; use different teaching practices and bring in the same assessment, or bring different types of assessments for the same teaching practice.) What student work are we going to bring to the next collaboration? What else will we do before the next meeting to improve in this area and help answer our question (e.g., conduct peer observations, read books and resources, attend trainings, have someone model a practice)?

 resources.corwin.com/ZwiersK3Guide

ASSESSMENT *AS* LEARNING: PEER AND SELF-ASSESSMENT

Many teachers and students have discovered the power of peer and self-assessment. This allows students to take more ownership over their learning and development of conversation skills and content understandings. You and your students can modify portions of the COAT to create student-friendly peer and self-assessment tools. You may start with a tool focused on nonverbal and listening skills. Then you add another tool focused on clarifying and supporting, and so on. Some teachers have triads meet during which one student is the coach who uses a tool to observe and provide feedback for the other two talking. Then they switch roles. Some samples of these tools are provided on the following pages.

These sample tools can be adapted by teachers for different developmental levels and language proficiencies.

Table 5.1   Sample Conversation: Self-Assessment

Criteria	Well	OK	Need to Improve
I clarified ideas and asked my partner to clarify ideas, when needed.			
I supported ideas with examples and evidence and asked my partner for support, when needed.			
We stayed focused on building an idea (or both ideas, one after the other, if an argument).			
I valued my partner's ideas and showed with my body and eyes that I was listening.			

online resources   resources.corwin.com/ZwiersK3Guide

Table 5.2   Sample Conversation: Peer Assessment

Questions	Notes for Feedback
How well did the two build up the first idea using clarifying and examples?	
How well did they use examples from the story?	
How well did they value one another's ideas?	
How hard did they try to explain their thoughts to one another?	
How even was their sharing? Did either student dominate the talk time?	
How well did they follow the prompt?	

online resources   resources.corwin.com/ZwiersK3Guide

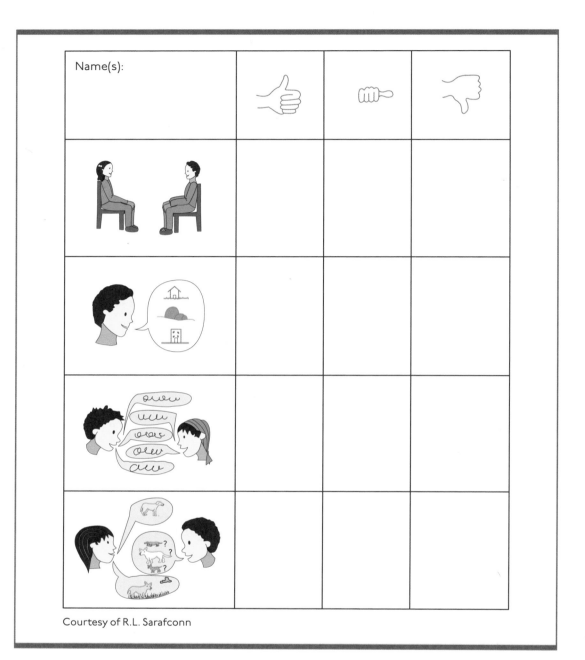

Name(s):	👍	✊	👎

Courtesy of R.L. Sarafconn

Figure 5.1   Sample Pictorial Peer and Self-Assessment for Conversations

online resources   resources.corwin.com/ZwiersK3Guide

Table 5.3 Sample Focused Listening and Nonverbal Communication Peer and Self-Assessment

Eye contact	Rarely	Sometimes	Often
Facing each other	Rarely	Sometimes	Often
Leaning toward each other	Rarely	Sometimes	Often
Nodding head to show understanding	Rarely	Sometimes	Often
Appropriate gestures and facial expressions	Rarely	Sometimes	Often
Uh, huh . . . Wow! Interesting Hmm . . .	Rarely	Sometimes	Often

Name:_____ Date:_____ Topic:_____

online resources resources.corwin.com/ZwiersK3Guide

ASSESSMENT *OF* LEARNING: SUMMATIVE ASSESSMENT OF CONVERSATIONS

The few teachers who dive into summative assessment of conversations tend to say it's worth the time and energy. First of all, it gives students something to shoot for as they talk during the semester or year. A teacher can pose a challenge: "At the end of the semester, I will record a conversation between you and a partner about a topic that we just studied. I will expect to hear effective use of conversation skills, thinking, academic language, and so on." With these objectives in mind, students have more purpose for practicing these things during the term. You can use the COAT or a variation of it to guide the practice conversations and to assess the final conversations.

You can choose the type of conversation that you want students to have. We tend to push for some form of argumentation because it tends to be more engaging and requires them to build up at least two ideas, not just one. Even if students lack sophistication in evaluating and comparing and choosing the two sides, they usually can have solid conversations that build up both ideas with clarifying and supporting skills. The conversations also offer windows into students' content learning, speaking, listening, thinking, and nonverbal communication skills. In their practice assessments, you can have triads in which a third student assesses and provides feedback to the two being observed. For argumentation, we have even seen students use the Argument Balance Scale (see Chapter 2) to support their conversations, while their teachers take assessment notes on the scale.

CHAPTER SUMMARY

This chapter offered a brief look at the wide world of assessing conversations. We zoomed in on assessment *for* learning and ended with assessment *of* learning, while all along, because of the power of conversations—even those being assessed—we were emphasizing "assessment *as* learning." There is much more to learn, and we have learned much about assessing conversations between our right now (writing this paragraph) and your right now (your reading of this paragraph). What we all must do is keep on tapping into the power of conversations for learning and seeing learning, and we must keep sharing those insights with one another.

PLC PROMPTS FOCUSED ON
ASSESSING ACADEMIC CONVERSATIONS

- Did you try the COAT in your classroom? How did it provide a window into your students' thinking?

- Share samples of students' self-assessments. How are they thinking meta-cognitively about their own learning and conversation skills?

- Do they value (and not disrespect) one another's ideas? How can we promote empathy, foster equity, and reduce bias?

APPENDIX A

How to Support Families in Helping Their Children Develop Conversation Skills

Families have many strengths to share, one of which is rich conversation. All family members can model nonverbal skills such as smiling, nodding, and making eye contact. All families can converse in their first languages, and despite the cultural differences between conversational styles and practices at home and those at school, there are many similar aspects that families can support at home. In this appendix, we explain ideas used at Brophy Elementary for involving families in academic and regular conversations.

SCHOOL EVENTS

One way to encourage interactions between family members, students, and teachers is to incorporate academic conversation skills in family-school events. For example, a special event was held for bilingual families in the school cafeteria. We set up centers that families could rotate through. One center had information about how to sign up for a summer program, another explained how to interpret standardized test scores, and a third center shared effective conversation skills. One of our third-grade students and her mother volunteered to serve as models and demonstrated how they talk about ideas at home. The focus was on active listening (eye contact, smiling, and nodding), paraphrasing, and elaborating. Then the families used binder rings and index cards for a "make and take" of conversation questions to keep handy for car rides or dinnertime. Prompts (written in the language of the home) included: "What is a favorite memory from your childhood?" "What do you want to be when you grow up?" "How are we similar and different?"

If families are invited to hear a speaker talk, be sure the speaker knows in advance that the lecture must include pauses for conversations. For example, our school is hosting a presentation on cyber safety. The speaker is an expert on the topic and has a lot of information to share. However, he can also pause and ask the parents to turn and talk to the person next to them. Ask, "How do you try to keep your child safe?" The participants can leave with a prompt to bring home to start a conversation with their child. "Have you ever heard of cyberbullying?" "Will you come to me for help if this happens to you?"

HOME-SCHOOL COMMUNICATION AND CONVERSATION-BASED HOMEWORK

Another successful method for promoting conversations at home is to include prompts in the weekly notice to families. Many teachers send a weekly or monthly bulletin to inform parents about the curriculum topics. This communication is sent in the home language and English. Typically, the bulletin might include, "In math we are learning to round to the nearest 10. In social studies we are learning the names of the continents." Several teachers included conversation prompts aligned with the topics and have gotten positive feedback from parents about this practice. Now, the bulletin reports, "In math we are learning to round to the nearest 10. Ask your child, 'When would you need to round to the nearest 10? Why?' In social studies we are learning the names of the continents. Ask your child, 'Which continent would you like to visit and why?'" By including a specific prompt, the parent will be able to ask the child a question that the child is prepared to answer. It is a great improvement on "What did you learn in school today?" (Typical response, "Nothing.")

IMPROVING SCHOOLING PRACTICES

Conversations between home and school have inspired teachers to improve the curriculum. An example of this is the radical shift in our school research fair in the third grade. In past years, the third graders all chose a famous person to research. Clara Barton, Anne Frank, and Alexander Graham Bell were all popular choices. Some famous Latinos were chosen, such as Sonia Sotomayor. Third graders read biographies, took notes, and created poster presentations about their famous person. On the day of the research fair, families came to school and toured the presentations. Students stood proudly by their projects, some dressed like the person they had studied. They answered questions from the visitors. Last year, we provided more support for parents, grandparents, and other relatives who came to the fair. We offered sentence starters and question starters in both Spanish and English to help increase interaction. "Can you elaborate . . . ?" *"Puedes elaborar . . . ?"* "I notice that . . ." *"Yo me doy cuenta de que . . ."* "Can you explain . . . ?" *"Puedes explicar . . ."* "I like how you . . ." *"Me gusta como tu . . ."* These promoted some increased interaction, but, while interesting, the biographical presentations were not as engaging as they could have been. The lack of ethnic and racial diversity in the choice of subjects was also concerning.

This year, we realized that many families have important stories to tell. The immigrant families in our community have overcome great obstacles to establish new beginnings. They have knowledge in the areas of music, construction, sales, household organization, and agriculture. These are stories that need to be recorded and shared. The third-grade teachers opened up the choices for students. Instead of studying famous people who have biographies available at a third-grade reading level, we now encourage students to interview their own family members or other members of our community. Students were able to explore their own identities through conversations with family members. One student interviewed her grandmother who is from Colombia. She brought in a small mill that is used to grind corn and an accompanying photograph of her *abuela* using the mill in Colombia. The girl wore a typical, colorful dress from the Antioquia region. During the annual research fair, family members and invited guests sat with students for in-depth conversations about their projects. Students answered questions about language, country of origin, customs, traditions, and important milestones. Through this project, we learned from each other.

Conversations connect, cultivate, create, and cross-pollinate.

APPENDIX B

Frequently Asked Questions

1. HOW DO I HAVE TIME TO IMPLEMENT ACADEMIC CONVERSATIONS?

Academic conversations can be incorporated into every subject area. For example, after independent reading, students can volunteer to give book talks about their books. After each student talks, another student can offer to paraphrase or retell what she or he said. Another student can ask an elaboration question (e.g., Which character do you like the best and why?). During social studies, students can ask each other in pairs which U.S. citizen right is most important and retell what their partners said. If there is time, teachers can have students practice conversations in class during snack time.

2. HOW CAN WE ACCELERATE THE TRANSFER OF CONVERSATION SKILLS INTO LITERACY?

Paraphrasing and/or retelling are skills students need to use on many types of reading assessments. One suggestion is to teach students to "talk in paragraphs": give a main idea and two or three supporting details every time you participate. Another suggestion is to have students engage in a written conversation in which they pass a paper back and forth.

3. HOW CAN I DESIGN A STUDENT LEARNING GOAL AND COLLECT DATA ON SKILL DEVELOPMENT?

Start by looking at these sample goals, which can be revised for your instructional setting.

- During this academic year, I will use language function frames to plan effective instruction focused on constructive conversations. The use of language functions will be observed during English language instruction and in general educational settings. Additionally, I will survey students for self-reported use of these functions (e.g., comparing, evaluating, supporting with evidence).

- During this academic year, I will record four paired student academic conversations. Together with my colleagues, we will analyze the conversations with the Conversation Observation and Analysis Tool (COAT). I will use peer feedback to reflect on and improve instruction for my students. The analysis will focus on how I promote student engagement and student-to-student interaction.

4. MY STUDENTS ARE NOT HAVING "DEEP" CONVERSATIONS. THEY ARE STUCK AT A SUPERFICIAL LEVEL. WHAT SHOULD I DO?

Share your challenges with your colleagues during collaboration time or team planning time. Your colleagues may be able to guide you to craft more engaging prompts or think of strategies that could motivate your students to reach higher levels of thinking. Use rubrics or a version of the COAT to assess student work and inform instruction. Model with a student volunteer the in-depth type of conversation that you are expecting. Provide a poster that includes academic phrases to deepen conversations. Ask for two volunteers to video record, and then as a whole class watch the conversation and provide compliments and feedback. (Use this step only if the two volunteers are willing.)

5. HOW CAN I IMPLEMENT PROFESSIONAL DEVELOPMENT IN MY SCHOOL AROUND ACADEMIC CONVERSATIONS?

A whole school initiative focused on academic conversations can be very effective. Find ways for staff in different roles to participate. Here is an example from the Brophy Elementary School in Framingham, Massachusetts. First, we provided books on academic conversations for the school data team. We introduced the purpose of academic conversations at a faculty meeting. Next, we wrote sample lesson plans and created anchor charts. These were presented to the school data team, who then shared back at grade-level meetings. A feature skill was introduced on a monthly basis. In the first year, we developed a two-credit course that was open to teachers and other staff. Classroom teachers, specialists (including music, art, and PE), and the school social worker all participated. Several of the grade-level teams began to implement use of the Protocol for Analyzing Academic Conversations (see Chapter 5) during their weekly grade-level meetings. The ability to choose an inquiry question and look at student work (conversations and then also written products) was a powerful change agent. Finally, the ELL coach engaged in coaching cycles with teachers across the school. This embedded coaching included a planning meeting, a co-teaching experience, and a debriefing. Teachers could request the coaching and include it in their professional practice goal.

---

online resources ⤢ | Visit the companion website at **resources.corwin.com/ZwiersK3Guide** for videos and downloadable resources.

References

Beck, I., McKeown, M., & Kucan, L. (2013). *Bringing words to life* (2nd ed.). New York, NY: Guildford.

Beeman, K., & Urow, C. (2012). *Teaching for biliteracy: Strengthening bridges between languages.* Philadelphia, PA: Caslon.

Calkins, L. (2010). *A guide to the reading workshop.* Portsmouth, NH: Heinemann.

Cole, A. D. (2003). *Knee to knee, eye to eye: Circling in on comprehension.* Portsmouth, NH: Heinemann.

Demi. (1996). *The empty pot.* Square Fish, Macmillan.

Farroni, T., Csibra, G., Simion, F., & Johnson, M. H. (2002, July). Eye contact detection in humans from birth. *Proceedings of the National Academy of Sciences, 99*(14), 9602–9605. DOI: 10.1073/pnas.152159999 PMCID: PMC12318

Fisher, D., Frey, N., & Rothenberg, C. (2008). *Content area conversations.* Alexandria, VA: ASCD.

Goldenberg, C. (1992). Instructional conversations: Promoting comprehension through discussion. *Reading Teacher, 46*(4), 316–326.

Gottlieb, M., & Willner, L. (2016, October 14). *Assessment equity for ELLs and ELLs with disabilities.* Paper presented at WIDA Conference, Philadelphia, PA.

Humphries, C., & Parker, R. (2015). *Making number talks matter: Developing mathematical practices and deepening understanding, grades 4–10.* Portland, ME: Stenhouse.

McIntyre, E., Kyle, D., & Moore, G. (2006). A primary-grade teacher's guidance toward small-group dialogue. *Reading Research Quarterly, 41*(1), 36–66.

Moses, L. (2015). *Supporting English learners in the reading workshop.* Portsmouth, NH: Heinemann.

Ritchhart, R., Church, M., & Morrison, K. (2011). *Making thinking visible: How to promote engagement, understanding, and independence for all learners.* San Francisco, CA: Jossey-Bass.

Singer, T., & Zwiers, J. (2016). What conversations can capture. In *Educational Leadership 73* (7). Retrieved from http://www.ascd.org/publications/educational-leadership/apr16/vol73/num07/What-Conversations-Can-Capture.aspx

Tierney, R. J. (2009). Agency and artistry of meaning makers within and across digital spaces. In S. Israel & G. Duffy (Eds.), *Handbook of Research on Reading Comprehension* (pp. 261–288). New York, NY: Guilford.

Wasik, B., & Iannone-Campbell, C. (2012). Developing vocabulary through purposeful, strategic conversations. *Reading Teacher, 66*(2), 321–332.

Zwiers, J., O'Hara, S., & Pritchard, R. (2014). *Common core standards in diverse classrooms.* Portland, ME: Stenhouse.

Zwiers, J., & Soto, I. (2016). *Academic language mastery: Conversational discourse in context.* Thousand Oaks, CA: Corwin.

Index

A SAGE Publishing Company

CORWIN HAS ONE MISSION: to enhance education through intentional professional learning.

We build long-term relationships with our authors, educators, clients, and associations who partner with us to develop and continuously improve the best evidence-based practices that establish and support lifelong learning.

Solutions you want. Experts you trust.
Results you need.